BERLITZ®

NORMANDY

5th edition (1994/1995)

How to use our guide

- All the **practical information,** hints and tips that you will need before or during your trip start on page 101.

- For **general background,** see the sections Normandy and the Normans, page 6, and A Brief History, page 13.

- All the **sights** to see in Normandy are listed between pages 27 and 84. Our own choice of sights most highly recommended is pinpointed by the Berlitz traveller symbol.

- **Sports, entertainment** and other **leisure activities** are analyzed between pages 85 and 91, while information on restaurants and cuisine is to be found on pages 91 to 100.

- Finally there is an **index** at the back of the book, pages 127 to 128.

Found an error or omission in this Berlitz guide? Or a change or new feature we should know about? Our editor would be happy to hear from you, and a postcard would do. Be sure to include your name and address, since in appreciation for a useful suggestion, we'd like to send you a free travel guide.

Although we make every effort to ensure the accuracy of all the information in this book, changes occur incessantly. We cannot therefore take responsibility for facts, prices, addresses and circumstances in general that are constantly subject to alteration.

Text: Jack Altman
Staff Editor: Christina Jackson
Layout: Doris Haldemann
Photography: Mireille Vautier;
　　　　　　　p. 19 Bibliothèque Municipale, ville de Bayeux;
　　　　　　　p. 61 PRISMA/Schuster GmbH
We wish to express our thanks to Nicholas Campbell and Adrienne Jackson for their help in the preparation of this guide.
Cartography: Falk-Verlag, Hamburg.

Contents

Cover photo: Trouville waterfront; *pp. 2–3:* Quiet moment on Trouville beach **5**

Normandy and the Normans

Normandy is rural France at its most civilized. It's the province that a cunning French king gave to the wild Norsemen—Normans—to get them to stop their plunder, rape and murder and settle down. The soil's comforting fertility tamed them, and they in turn shaped the forests and meadows to the green and pleasant land that to-day offers the serenest of holidays to the modern visitor.

An enormous charm but nothing very wild about latter-

day Normandy. The coastline along the English Channel has little of the wind-buffeted ruggedness of Brittany. As Paris's most convenient playground, the coast is best known for the genteel Channel resorts, with their grand hotels still offering a distant hint of the *Belle Epoque*, at Deauville, Houlgate and Cabourg or, on the west coast of the Cotentin peninsula, Carteret, Coutainville and Granville. Even the dramatic cliffs of Etretat have achieved a

Normandy's subtle play of colour: the yellow of the colza fields or the silver grey of Honfleur slate.

reassuring familiarity as a picturesque framework for the resort's tranquil little shingle beach.

Inland, the eastern half of the province, known as Haute-Normandie (Upper Normandy), is the seat of its rich industrialized agriculture: vast fields of wheat, sugar beet and flax flourish in the Pays de Caux between the north coast and the Seine river, in the Vexin on the edge of the Paris basin, and on the Neubourg plain south of the Seine river.

Meandering through Normandy from Paris to its estuary at Le Havre, the Seine is vital as the capital's only link with the sea. Ocean-going vessels still come upriver to Rouen to make it the country's fourth most important commercial port (after Marseille, Le Havre and Dunkerque). Rouen's industries—textiles, chemicals, paper and petroleum products—depend on the raw materials brought in through the port. Enhanced by many beautiful beech and oak forests, the river valley has little agriculture along its banks except for a few orchards closer to Paris, between Vernon and Gaillon, and some cattle pastures around the estuary.

Haute-Normandie is completed, on its eastern edge in the Pays de Bray, by that characteristic Norman landscape—the patchwork of rolling green meadows surrounded by hedgerows and embankments of trees—known as *bocage*.

The *bocage* is the dominant feature of Basse-Normandie (Lower Normandy), which comprises the west and centre of the old province. It's the meadows and orchards of the Pays d'Auge south of Lisieux that produce the bulk of Normandy's glory, the great cheeses—Livarot, Pont-l'Evêque and Camembert—and the cider and Calvados apple brandy. Normandy's agricultural growth over the last few centuries owes much to the proximity of the national capital and the need to supply its ever-increasing appetite for meat and dairy products.

The province is also renowned for two breeds of horse: the powerful Percheron carthorse, cherished since the Crusades and still bred at Louis XV's Haras du Pin stables, and the sleek Thoroughbred, which can be seen in the August yearling sales at Deauville.

Examining the net profits at the Channel port of Fécamp.

There's nothing you could really call a mountain here. But that doesn't stop them, with a rare example of Norman humour, naming one of their slightly more elevated regions the Suisse Normande (Norman Switzerland) and a southern range of hills, with its Mont des Avaloirs soaring dizzily up to 417 metres (1,368 ft.), the Alpes Mancelles. The rolling hills of the Suisse Normande, south of Caen, rise all of 200 metres (650 ft.), but densely wooded ravines along the valley of the Orne river make it lovely country in its own right, even if the cows don't wear bells around their necks.

You don't get all this greenery without a little rain. If you were to average Normandy's rainy days throughout the year, it would work out at one day in two. But in fact, the showers come in short clusters, in summer perhaps four days in a row before a couple of weeks of uninterrupted brilliant sunshine. As a rule, the spring can be risky, although the May blossom is spectacular; July less rainy than August; early autumn best of all. The constantly varying climate, all too familiar to Britons, encourages plenty of activity.

If, for the most part, man has left his respectful mark over practically every square inch of the Normandy countryside, his cities here are also high points of French civilization. And that despite terrible destruction during the cruel Battle of Normandy at the end of World War II.

Restored from the heavy bombardment, Rouen's cathedral and other monuments of Gothic church architecture rise in the middle of a prosperous old town of characteristic timbered Norman Renaissance houses. Caen suffered even more after the nearby Allied landings, but its grand Abbaye-aux-Hommes, built by William the Conqueror, still stands proud.

From Ouistreham to Sainte-Mère-Eglise, the D-Day beaches remain a major place of pilgrimage for old soldiers, their relatives and anyone at all moved by the great courage of the Allied forces who delivered France from the Germans. Bayeux's rapid liberation spared it destruction, and its famous 900-year-old tapestry survives intact to relate the saga of William's conquest of England.

Perhaps the most sublime monument to man's domination of the elements in Normandy is fashioned from the granite rocks of its Chausey Islands: the Mont-Saint-Michel's abbey rising out of the sea at the bottom of the Cotentin peninsula. Other abbeys, which suffered not so much from war as from the greed of profiteers after the French Revolution, stand in poignant ruined beauty at Jumièges, le Bec-Hellouin and Saint-Wandrille.

The prosperity of Normandy's long-established farmers, veritable squires in the old English sense, is reflected in their grandiose residences, often fortified manors rather than simple farmhouses, complete with moat, ramparts and turrets around a formidable but elegant edifice of brick, stone and cross-beamed timbering.

The commercial and industrial ports of Dieppe, Le Havre and Cherbourg make up in vigour for what they might lack in charm, but a more romantic taste for sailing and fishing ports can be delightfully rewarded at Fécamp, Honfleur, Ouistreham and Granville.

Normandy has been a fertile soil for many of France's leading painters, from Nicolas Poussin to Fernand Léger. The picture that gave its name to the revolutionary Impressionist movement, *Impression, soleil levant* (Impression, Rising Sun), was painted by Claude Monet from a boarding-house window overlooking the harbour at Le Havre. He was equally fascinated by the cliffs at Etretat and the hazy outlines he perceived in Rouen's cathedral. At Honfleur, Eugène Boudin was Monet's precursor and mentor, while Raoul Dufy captured the colourful festivities of Deauville's high society. The province has been no less important to great writers such as Gustave Flaubert and Guy de Maupassant, and Marcel Proust in search of time lost at the Grand Hotel in Cabourg.

Normandy's 3 million inhabitants have an age-old reputation for prudence. Perhaps ever since those Viking Norsemen decided to give up piracy and take up farming and commerce, caution has been the better part of their valour. The *réponse normande* (Norman answer) is a time-honoured way out of a sticky situation. Even if you merely ask whether it'll rain today, you may be told, with the assurance that you've just been handed a piece of profound wisdom: *"Peut-être bien que oui, peut-être bien que non"* (Maybe yes, maybe no).

You'll find Normans mostly quiet-spoken, polite but wary with strangers, yet very friendly once you've reassured them you won't be disturbing the normal rhythm of their lives. **11**

With few large towns but hundreds of little villages and hamlets, the rural character of the people is still strong, even among those who have, increasingly, migrated to the cities.

Norman cuisine is faithful to its traditional recipes, making plentiful use of cream and butter, cider and Calvados in the sauces. And an attachment to the sea remains in the custom, more persistent than in most regions of France, of a fish course preceding the meat —and separated by a quick glass of Calvados said to stimulate your appetite.

Does it? *"Peut-être bien que oui, peut-être bien que non."*

It's no fun being led by the nose to Bricquebec market, particularly if, like me, you know what's at stake.

A Brief History

With no mountain barriers to keep invaders out, the Normandy region has at all times been open to anyone tempted by its green and fertile land.

Danubians, Mediterraneans, Celts and Belgians, all types came to fish along its coasts, to hunt in the forests, and later to clear the woodlands for the earliest of France's farms.

Roman Control

In their conquest of Gaul, the Romans, for whom the region was just a north-eastern extension of Brittany (Armorica, as they called it), found the inhabitants valiantly resisting

---

Facts and Figures

Although much of the information given below can be found in various sections of the guide, key facts are grouped here for a quick briefing.

Political Divisions:	The province of Normandy, which corresponds more or less to the boundaries of the duchy established in the 10th century, is no longer a political unity. It is divided up administratively into two regions, Haute-Normandie and Basse-Normandie, which in turn are made up of *départements*: Eure and Seine-Maritime in Haute-Normandie, and Calvados, Orne and Manche in Basse-Normandie.
Geography:	The old province occupies the north-western region of France and is bounded to the north by the English Channel, to the west by Brittany, to the south by the Loire Valley and to the east by the Ile-de-France and Picardy. Haute-Normandie covers the eastern part of the province, Basse-Normandie the western and central part.
Area:	Haute-Normandie 12,317 sq. km. (4,803 sq. mi.); Basse-Normandie 17,589 sq. km. (6,858 sq. mi.).
Population:	Haute-Normandie 1,650,000; Basse-Normandie 1,318,000.
Principal Cities:	Haute-Normandie: Rouen (capital), pop. 380,000; Le Havre, pop. 254,000 Basse-Normandie: Caen (capital) 181,000

The main church of Jumièges abbey was consecrated in 1067, celebrating William's conquest of England.

from fortified settlements along the Channel coast and inland along the banks of the Seine. A local chieftain, Viridorix, led an important contingent in the last Gallic stand against Julius Caesar at Alesia, in Burgundy, in 52 B.C.

The Gallo-Romans established three important port cities along the Seine river and estuary—Caracotinum (Harfleur), Juliobona (Lillebonne) and Rotomagus (Rouen)—for trade with England. Minerals, especially lead, came in from Bristol and Southampton in exchange for wine, olive oil and other southern goods that came up from the Rhône and Saône rivers.

With a foundation of stone, a brick base and timbered walls with plaster filling, the Roman houses drew on local Celtic huts for their gabled shape—unmistakable forerunners of the classic Norman house of today.

Attacks by Germanic tribes from the east and north—Goths, Alamans and Franks—broke Roman control of the region in the 3rd and 4th centuries A.D.

Christian Beginnings

Christianity made its entry with bishoprics at Rouen and Bayeux, and the region all the more readily accepted the rule of Frankish king Clovis when he converted in 496. Other Christian dioceses sprang up in Avranches, Evreux, Sées, Coutances and Lisieux. Early

bishops were beatified, not from Rome but by popular local acclaim—Saint Taurin at Evreux, Saint Martin-des-Champs at Avranches.

Under the Merovingian dynasty, the region was divided into county-like territorial units known as *pagus* or *pays*—Caux, Vexin, Cotentin, etc.—that continued administratively right up to the French Revolution of 1789 and survive in popular parlance to this day.

The monastic traditions of Irish Saint Columba and the Roman Benedictines influenced the establishment of powerful abbeys, first at Rouen, then at Saint-Wandrille, Jumièges and **15**

Fécamp in the 7th century. In addition to their cultural and scholastic role, they constituted important economic enterprises, administering vineyards in the Poitou, olive groves down in the Rhône valley and Charlemagne's customs offices on his empire's northern frontier.

The Normans Arrive

At the end of the 8th century, fierce dragon-headed longships from the north made an appearance off the west coast of France on their way down from England and Ireland. The Vikings raided a few Channel ports, massacred the fisherfolk and disappeared.

They returned in force in 841 on a three-week raid up the Seine river which left Rouen and Jumièges in flames. Saint-Wandrille monastery survived by paying them to go away, and a delegation from Saint-Denis, north of Paris, came to buy the freedom of 68 hostages. Four years later, the boats reached Paris. The Vikings made it a yearly habit, arriving in spring, staging lightning summer raids inland on horseback, and withdrawing with their booty and prisoners in the autumn.

Two groups of Scandinavian Norsemen (Northmen or Normans) formed an uneasy alliance. The Danes, fleeing Carolingian expansion in the north and hearing that French monks had lots of gold and little defences, just wanted to take the money and run. The Norwegians were mostly aristocratic freebooters seeking to settle and breed cattle or build new fishing fleets.

In 911, Rollo, a Norwegian earl at the head of a predominantly Danish band that had rampaged through Scotland and France, was finally defeated at Chartres by Charles the Simple. The not so simple French king drew up a peace treaty that persuaded Rollo to give up this pillaging nonsense, become a good Christian (baptized as Robert) and set up home at Rouen, with the surrounding lands to be known as the Duchy of Normandy. In exchange, Duke Robert, now a feudal vassal to the French king, would stop other Vikings causing any more threats to the lands of the Paris basin known as the Ile-de-France.

Over the next 20 years, the duchy expanded to include the Bessin, the Cotentin peninsula and the Avranches country that had been in Breton hands (including the Mont-Saint-Michel), completing the historic boundaries of Normandy.

With a Frankish clergy and

administration, the Normans soon demonstrated their aptitude to assimilate the local culture as they did in their other wanderings around the world. They adopted French law and language, with only a few Nordic words creeping in, notably nautical such as *tribord* (starboard), *bâbord* (port) or *quille* (keel).

One Nordic law they did retain was that of banishment, whereby incorrigible plunderers were sent off on crusades and such, turning up in Sicily, Palestine or, closer to home, paving the way for future conquest in England. The Normans also continued polygamy and concubinage, producing a plethora of sons to place in key positions in the church and secular hierarchy across the Channel.

William the Conqueror

One such concubine was a Falaise tanner's daughter who had caught the eye of Duke Robert the Magnificent. After Robert's death on a Crusade in 1035, their son, William the Bastard, became the much disputed heir to the throne.

To fight off his rivals, William hoped to form an alliance with French king Henri I by marrying his niece, Matilda. But when William defeated the rebel barons and created a new aristocracy, his duchy was suddenly too strong, too independent for Henri's taste. Normandy had to resist a two-pronged attack from the king's army to the east and from royal allies along the southern border in Anjou.

Meanwhile, William was strengthening his links with England. With the English throne threatened by civil wars, the future King Edward the Confessor had sought refuge in Rouen, where he received a French education and surrounded himself with Norman advisors. He went back to claim his throne in 1042, accompanied by the Abbot of Jumièges (later Archbishop of Canterbury). In 1050, the heirless king asked for military help from William in exchange for what the Duke of Normandy understood to be a promise of the English throne at Edward's death.

As is recounted in the Bayeux Tapestry (see p. 56), Edward's rival, Harold, pledged to support William's claim but took the crown for himself. William gathered a fleet at Dives (near modern Cabourg) and made his way along the coast to wait in the Somme estuary until favourable winds took him across the Channel to his momentous victory at Hastings on October 14, 1066. Heading an army of Bretons, Normans and French mercenaries, the Bastard was henceforth known as the Conqueror.

William was crowned King of England at Westminster Abbey on Christmas Day, but returned to Normandy four months later to show off the rich booty of gold, silver and jewellery at a celebration banquet at Fécamp and to strengthen the duchy with his new prestige.

His Norman lords owned lands on both sides of the Channel, bequeathing their more highly prized Norman lands to the first son and the English lands to the second. Thus, at William's death in 1087, oldest son Robert was given the duchy, while kid brother William Rufus had to make do with England.

France Takes Charge

While the Norman dukes owed feudal allegiance to the French

king, they linked their administration and fortunes to those of England rather than France. After 20 years of turmoil following the iron-fisted rule of William the Conqueror, Henry I reunited the titles of King of England and Duke of Normandy, and when grandson Henry II married Eleanor of Aquitaine in 1152, Normandy became part of a state that stretched from Scotland down to the Pyrenees. The French king felt threatened.

Richard the Lion-Heart had constantly to fight his cousin and fellow-crusader King Philippe Auguste for control of Normandy's eastern domains bordering the Ile-de-France. To win Philippe's approval of him as Richard's successor, weak and greedy John was forced to give up the Vexin and Evreux.

Clumsily stealing a vassal's betrothed as his own bride, John gave the French king the ideal pretext to invade the duchy in 1203. The following year, Philippe captured the strategically vital fortress of Château Gaillard on the Seine and annexed the whole of Normandy for the French crown.

The French kings preferred at first not to interfere with the duchy's tradition of strong autonomy within the feudal system. It had created an efficient administration, prosperous agriculture—wheat, barley and rye—and a burgeoning textile industry from home-grown flax and hemp and vegetable dyes of weld (yellow), woad (blue) and madder (red).

Although the Norman mer-

Action-packed Bayeux Tapestry brings history vividly to life.

Joan at the Stake

It was in Rouen that Joan of Arc was tried as "schismatic, apostate, liar, witch, heretic and blasphemer"—charges drawn up by professors of the University of Paris. The established order felt threatened by her highly personal religious experience of hearing, without Church help, the saints' voices exhorting her to lead the French against the English. Jobs were at stake.

To the English, she was a meddling morale-booster who seemed to be giving the hitherto feeble French army just enough backbone to boot them out of France. So, when she finally fell into English hands in 1430 after being captured at Compiègne, they had to find a means of getting rid of her.

Pierre Cauchon, Bishop of Beauvais hoping to get the vacant archbishopric of Rouen, was her chief judge and inquisitor. With the threat of burning her at the stake, he got Joan to give up her sinful men's clothing and sign a document denying the saints' voices and vowing submission to the Church.

But the English wanted her out of the way, so she was thrown back into prison where, to protect herself from her jailers, she had to don men's clothing again. She further proved she was an incorrigible heretic by retracting her denial of the voices. On May 30, 1431, she was burned at the stake on Rouen's Place du Vieux-Marché.

Happy endings: Joan's martyrdom inspired the French to boot the English out anyway, Cauchon didn't become archbishop, and Joan became, in 1920, a saint.

---

chant fleet was now constantly at war with the English, business flourished, with Rouen protected from competition with Paris by special privileges for its river trade. The prosperity encouraged a building boom: new cathedrals at Rouen and Coutances, and the abbey buildings known as the Mont-Saint-Michel's *Merveille*.

But King Louis IX and his successors wanted some of this wealth for their treasury. In 1281, in protest against taxes and the finagling exemptions and profiteering of the lords and bourgeoisie, the mayor of Rouen was assassinated, notables molested and their houses ransacked.

With the duke named from among the French royal family, Normandy became a constant source of dynastic struggles. Each claimant plundered and skirmished his way through the towns while the Normans took the day-to-day administration into their own hands.

Return of the English

As in most other French provinces at this time, Normandy's leaders reacted out of self-interest rather than any sense of "national" pride. When the Anglo-French Hundred Years' War broke out in the 14th century—over disputes of feudal allegiance involving Aquitaine and other territories—the Norman nobility and bourgeoisie readily collaborated with the English invaders rather than join the French cause south of the Loire. The English guaranteed them a profitable percentage from tax collecting, secure maritime trade, and high office with which to hold on to their lands.

Bearing the brunt of the soldiers' pillaging and the new taxes, the common people were understandably more anti-English. Rouen courts made it a punishable offence to use the swear-word *fils d'Anglais* (son of an Englishman). English seamen trying to "colonize" Honfleur were driven home by local hostility.

The Mont-Saint-Michel, the only piece of Normandy to withstand enemy occupation,

Rouen's old clock has been keeping time for centuries.

became the symbol of resistance from 1424, when the monks helped organize a small garrison to fend off a 10-year English siege of their abbey- **21** fortress. The archangel Michael duly became the patron saint of the national revolt and appeared in Poitou in 1429 to talk to Joan of Arc.

Spoiled by their privileged treatment during the English occupation, the Norman barons were distinctly uppity towards the French king after the Hundred Years' War. Louis XI's brother, Duke Charles, led them in a rebellious alliance with the Duke of Brittany. The king crushed the revolt in 1466 and, three years later, ceremonially smashed the duke's symbolic ring of office, putting an end to Normandy's special status as a duchy.

Renaissance and Revolution

Normandy's political independence was gone for good but the post-war reconstruction brought a new prosperity. This time it favoured the peasantry and a landed gentry emerging from among the urban bourgeoisie that gradually replaced the humiliated aristocracy.

A flourish of Flamboyant Gothic and elegant Renaissance building expressed the new mood of the 16th century: Rouen cathedral's Tour de Beurre, the nearby Saint-Maclou and Palais de Justice, the Bishop of Evreux's palace and the Mont-Saint-Michel's new chancel.

With an enlightened reform-minded clergy at the University of Caen and help forthcoming from Protestant England, the province provided a more or less safe haven for Henri IV and his Huguenots in the Wars of Religion against the Catholic League. But, always aware of which way the wind was blowing, the Normans installed a Jesuit college at Caen in 1609, a year before Henri IV's assassination, and the Protestants were abandoned.

The lucrative maritime trade —principally with England, but also with the Netherlands and south-western France—overwhelmingly benefited the eastern ports (Dieppe, Le Tréport, Fécamp, Le Havre, Honfleur and Rouen), while the west (Basse-Normandie) had to settle for fishing and local trade.

Normandy's privileged position as the distribution centre for Britain's wood, cattle, leather, cloth and raw materials such as coal, lead and tin, came to a halt when the Industrial Revolution enabled the British to dispense with the continent's labour and manufacturing skills. Rouen responded at the end of the 17th century with its own cotton and linen manufacturing, forming a textile triangle with Elbeuf and Louviers, but the province's economy was in general decline under the burden of increased taxes to finance the wars of Louis XIV and his successors.

Normandy's farming at this time was mostly in dairy cattle and fruit orchards, with cider replacing the wines of the failing Seine valley vineyards. Little use was made of new agricultural techniques, the gentlemen farmers being more interested in landscaping English-style gardens than expanding their arable land.

With the gentry showing traditional prudence, Normandy took very much of a back seat in the French Revolution. However, during the British blockade of the main coastal ports of Le Havre and Cherbourg, the Normans rediscovered their ancient skills as pirates, sailing from Dieppe, Granville and Honfleur.

The Prussian occupation of Normandy following Napoleon's defeat was mercifully brief, as the soldiers billeted on the local population near Pont-Audemer were each entitled to a litre of Calvados per day.

The Nineteenth Century

The boom of France's own belated but vigorous industrial revolution greatly benefited the textiles of Normandy. Steamships brought Channel and transatlantic trade up the Seine.

The railways made a characteristically cautious and hesitant start, profiting in large part from British knowhow; English-language newspapers, *The Norman Times* and *The Railway Advocate and Continental Express*, were even published in Rouen for the construction teams.

The new lines from Paris to the coast were the prime instigator of a vital new industry—tourism. When the Duchess of Berry, leaning prudently on the arm of the sub-prefect of Dieppe, dipped a toe in the water in 1824, she launched a fashion for sea-bathing. Previously, sea water had been recommended only as a cure for rabies bites.

Alexandre Dumas, preferring sandy beaches to pebbles, made Trouville more popular than Dieppe. The Duke of Morny's building speculation attracted Napoleon III's aristocrats and upstarts to neighbouring Deauville. The influx of new money had its influence on local politics, with the mayor of the Catholic pilgrimage town of Lisieux losing ground to the mayor of Deauville with his pagan but lucrative casino.

Wars and Peace

Normandy was untouched by the fighting in World War I, but Rouen was a base for British, Canadian and U.S. supplies, and troops from India, Australia and Canada camped in the Cotentin and the *département* of Seine-Maritime.

After the invasion of France in 1940, Normandy served as Germany's western base to prepare the assault on England. While troops trained for disembarkation on the Channel cliffs, bombing raids were launched from Normandy air bases. The catastrophic 1942 Canadian raid on Dieppe, without adequate air and naval support, showed the Allies the vital need for meticulous preparations (over 18 months) for the D-Day landings. After weeks of diversionary bombings, the first Allied parachutists landed during the night of June 5–6, 1944, to take up positions at the eastern base of the Cotentin peninsula and on the Orne estuary, at either end of the beaches designated for Operation Overlord—as the invasion was dubbed.

At 6.30 a.m., the first of a fleet of 4,266 vessels landed —British and Canadians on beaches code-named Sword, Juno and Gold and the Ameri-

Peace reigns anew over Normandy after sacrifices of World War II.

cans on Omaha and Utah. While the British were able to instal their artificial Mulberry harbour at Arromanches (see p. 58) to land tanks, artillery and other equipment, atrocious weather and tough German resistance bogged the Americans down in fierce fighting before they could push on to liberate their region.

Bayeux was the first town to be freed, on June 7, unscathed, but Caen, Rouen and scores of other towns and villages were ravaged by Allied and German bombing in the bitter Battle of Normandy that ended only on August 21.

Peacetime has been a blessedly uneventful story: prosperous industrial reconstruction, large-scale agribusiness and ever-growing tourism boosted by the Autoroute de Normandie which in 1977 linked Paris with Rouen and Caen.

Historical Landmarks

Prehistory	3600 B.C.	Danubian settlement in Calvados.
	300	Belgians migrate into Normandy.
Roman Gaul	58–50	Roman conquest of Gaul.
	42 A.D.	Claudius includes Normandy in Breton Armorica.
Christianization	250	Mellon first Bishop of Rouen.
	649–54	Saint-Wandrille and Jumièges monasteries established.
	708	The Mont-Saint-Michel founded.
Norman Invasions	841	Viking raid on Seine.
	911	French king gives Norsemen Duchy of Normandy.
	1035–87	William the Conqueror is Duke of Normandy.
	1066	Norman conquest of England.
French Control	1204	King John defeated; Normandy annexed to France.
Hundred Years' War	1417–50	English occupation.
	1431	Joan of Arc executed at Rouen.
Royal Normandy	1589–90	Henri IV defeats Catholics at battles of Arques and Ivry.
	1755	Rouen builds France's first cotton-spinning machine.
19th Century	1815	Prussian occupation after defeat of Napoleon.
	1824	Duchess of Berry at Dieppe beach launches tourist industry.
	1843–48	Railway from Paris to Rouen; extended to Le Havre.
World War II	1942	Canadian raid on Dieppe.
	1944	D-Day landings.

Where to Go

By taking advantage of the excellent network of roads, you can switch easily between Normandy's greenery and the coastal resorts and enjoy both the first-rate sporting facilities and the rich cultural heritage of its monuments.

Shell-fishing at Houlgate usually turns up more shells than fish.

If you are coming from England on the Newhaven-Dieppe car-ferry, you will have a chance to explore the north-east coast before heading for Rouen and the Seine valley. From Paris, the Autoroute de Normandie (A13) takes you along the Seine to Rouen before cutting across to Deauville and neighbouring seaside resorts and continuing further west to Caen.

But Normandy is best visited at a leisurely pace, away from

the *autoroute*, along the country lanes. For overnight stays, you'll very often be better off steering clear of the towns in favour of the many delightful country inns that Normandy specializes in—converted watermills, manors, farmhouses or luxurious châteaux.

Our selection of sights is by no means exhaustive—but certainly exhausting if you try to do it all on one trip. The secret of enjoying Normandy is tasting its variety. Don't overdose on the cultural monuments without an occasional dip in the sea, and get off the beach from time to time for a walk in those marvellous forests.

The Seine Valley

From its dominant position on the Seine, midway between Paris and the coast, Rouen makes an ideal start to your tour. It is surrounded by cliff-top vantage points—from which to admire the Seine valley—and forests for pleasant

hikes and picnics. Within easy reach to the east is the gentle countryside of the Pays de Bray, with the artistic pilgrimage spot of Claude Monet's house at Giverny, and the cathedral town of Evreux to the south.

To the west is the "Route des Abbayes" through the gentle green countryside of Normandy's medieval abbeys, many of them in ruin, quiet places for a moment's repose.

Rouen

The historic Norman capital's civic pride breathes from every stone and timber frame lovingly restored or reconstructed after the crippling bomb damage of 1944. After all, this is the ancient centre of Normandy's thriving textile industry and the place of Joan of Arc's martyrdom—a symbol of national resistance to tyranny.

Hugging a loop in the Seine, the town did draw at least one advantage from the war—the factories on the left bank were destroyed, leaving room for a modern residential area, while the industries were rebuilt on

The moated manor at Coupesarte is no idle monument but centrepiece of a highly active farm. **31**

the outskirts. On the right bank, the charming medieval and Renaissance centre around the cathedral has been renovated and is now for pedestrians only.

Start your walk, not at the cathedral, but at the western end of the historic district, on the **Place du Vieux-Marché**. Old and new Rouen come together here around the bright and airy market halls (great selection of cheese and fruit) and the imposing modern **Église Sainte-Jeanne-d'Arc**. Nearby is a monument marking the spot where Joan was burned at the stake in 1431. Some stones from the rostrum of her judges have been excavated. Only a few Frenchmen still bear a grudge against the British (notably when it comes to negotiating agricultural prices for the European Community), but ironic remarks should be avoided—the French take their freedom fighters seriously. Inside the church are some dazzling 16th-century **stained-glass windows** salvaged from an older church bombed in 1944.

Leading south-east from the market is Rouen's most celebrated street, the **Rue du Gros-Horloge**, now as always the city's bustling commercial centre. Its timber-framed houses of the 15th, 16th and 17th centuries are splendid examples of sturdy Norman architecture, achieving a very pleasing irregularity in the way the plaster is set in oblique and rectangular forms between the solid oak beams. The elegant Renaissance arched clock-tower of the **Gros-Horloge** is the town's emblem. The ornamental gilded clock face has only the hour hand.

Beside the clock is a 14th-century belfry which still rings its bell at 9 p.m., time of the old curfew. Take the spiral staircase to the roof for a view of the city and its circle of hills around the Seine valley.

East of the Gros-Horloge stands the great **Cathédrale Notre-Dame**, made famous in the modern age by Monet's many Impressionist studies of its façade. The asymmetry of the two towers embracing the delicate tracery of the slender spires between them creates a highly original silhouette among France's best-loved cathedrals.

The **façade** offers a remarkably harmonious anthology of Gothic architecture. The north tower, Tour Saint-Romain, has the sober simplicity of the cathedral's early Gothic beginnings in the 12th century, while the taller and **33** more elaborate south tower, Tour de Beurre, is Flamboyant Gothic of the 15th century. (According to local belief, this "Butter Tower" was paid for by Catholic burghers in exchange for a papal dispensation from giving up good Normandy butter during Lent.)

Similarly, the austerely sculpted porches flanking the main entrance are from the early period, while the more ornamental elongated central porch and the gabled upper windows were added in the 15th and 16th centuries. The main steeple is neo-Gothic of the 19th century.

The rather severe interior contrasts with the elaborate exterior, but the impact of its double-storeyed nave is lightened by the tall arches of the choir. In the Chapelle de la Vierge beyond the choir is the monumental Renaissance **tomb of the Cardinals of Amboise**, with superbly sculpted allegories of the cardinal virtues. On the south side of the choir is the more modest tomb of the most heroic of medieval English kings, portrayed recumbent above the inscription in Latin: "Here is buried the heart of King Richard of England, known as the Lion-Hearted."

Behind the cathedral, cross over the Rue de la République to the 15th-century **Eglise Saint-Maclou**, the richest example of Flamboyant Gothic in the country. Note the masterful Renaissance carving of the oak doors on the central and north portals. In the interior, the same exuberant artistry can be admired in the carved wood organ frame and the stone tracery of the spiral staircase.

Aître Saint-Maclou (184 Rue Martainville, near the church) is an impressive 16th-century atrium of buildings with timbered galleries, home of the school of fine arts. They once surrounded the parish cemetery, as can be seen from the carvings of the grave-diggers' tools and figures from the Dance of Death.

Back at the Eglise Saint-Maclou, turn north on **Rue Damiette**, graced by some of the town's handsomest old houses. The street leads to the elegant 14th-century Gothic abbey church, **Abbatiale Saint-Ouen**, with its splendid flying buttresses, best observed from the little park east of the chancel.

The Flamboyant Gothic steeple at Saint-Ouen looms over Rouen's medieval centre.

But go inside, too, to appreciate the atmosphere of lightness and grace achieved in the soaring proportions of the nave.

The last great monument of the old town, in the Rue aux Juifs, is the grand **Palais de Justice**, a jewel of Renaissance and Flamboyant Gothic architecture built on the site of the medieval ghetto. Recent excavations uncovered a 12th-century synagogue, one of the oldest in Europe (visits by arrangement with the Office de Tourisme, Place de la Cathédrale).

The prosperous town has a well-endowed **Musée des Beaux-Arts** (Square Verdrel), with important works by Velázquez, Caravaggio, Perugino, Veronese and Rubens. French artists include François Clouet, Delacroix and Rouen-born Théodore Géricault, who is represented by a series of dramatic paintings of horses.

The **Musée de la Céramique** (Rue Faucon) displays masterpieces of Rouen china-manufacturers from their heyday in the reigns of Louis XIV and XV. The richly ornamented tableware replaced the gold and silver plate melted down to finance the royal wars.

A remarkable collection of wrought iron—from elaborate balconies to locks and keys— can be found at the **Musée Le Secq-des-Tournelles** in the old Eglise Saint-Laurent. Important exhibits include the grill from the Abbaye d'Ourscamps and a music lectern from Amiens.

Rouen's most celebrated son is undoubtedly writer Gustave Flaubert, but they didn't like each other. When he was sued for the "immorality" of his greatest novel, *Madame Bovary*, the good burghers prayed that he would be properly punished for a book that so cruelly depicted the narrow-mindedness of the city in which he grew up.

His father, Achille-Cléophas Flaubert, was a surgeon at the municipal hospital, and the **Musée Flaubert** (furniture and other memorabilia in the family house at 51, Rue de Lecat) is also a museum of the history of medicine.

Forêt de Lyons

This magnificent forest of venerable beech and oak trees, one of the finest in the country, was a royal hunting reserve dating back to the Merovingian kings.

Start your excursion southeast of Rouen at the **Côte des Deux-Amants** (Hill of the Two Lovers). At the top there is a delightful picnic spot on a pla-eau surrounded by woods, with a panoramic view over the steep chalk cliffs of the Seine valley. The lovers? Hunter Raoul and Caliste, a lord's daughter whom he saved from a wild boar. To win her hand in marriage, he had to carry her up the hill in his arms. Raoul died from the effort, Caliste died of a broken heart and they were buried together on top of the hill. For modern lovers, there's a hill-top car park, and the plateau is an easy five-minute walk.

Cross over the Andelle river at PONT-SAINT-PIERRE and drive along the north bank to the bizarre ruins of an old cotton mill, the **Filature Levasseur**. Burned out a few weeks after its inauguration in 1870, it is built like a neo-Gothic cathedral, mostly of austere industrial red brick now gracefully clothed in ivy, its great ghostly "nave" resounding to the caws of crows and the barking of a hungry guard dog. The architect took his inspiration—and much of his masonry—from the nearby **Abbaye de Fontaine-Guérard**, also now in ruins. The remains of the elegant 13th-century monastery surround a spring still quietly gushing its healing waters.

In the middle of the forest, the sleepy village of **Lyons-la-Forêt**, with characteristic timbered Norman houses built around a 17th-century market hall, is ideal as an overnight base. South along the D715, the ruined **Abbaye de Mortemer** hugs the grassy slope of a valley beside the Fouillebroc trout stream. Its monks tended the forest to provide fuel for the local glass-blowing industry.

Pays de Bray

This cheerful countryside of woods and meadows, with an excursion circuit clearly signposted "Promenade dans le Pays de Bray", constitutes Normandy's historic frontier with the Paris basin (Ile-de-France).

Guarding the southern approaches, **Gisors** has made a lovely park out of the massive ramparts and towers of the **château fort** (fortress) built by William Rufus, son of the Conqueror, and expanded by Philippe Auguste. This strategically vital stronghold was a perennial bone of contention between the dukes of Normandy and the King of France till the end of the Hundred Years' War. The remarkable Gothic and Renaissance church, **Eglise Saint-Gervais-et-Saint-Protais**, has been restored to its former glory and is well worth a visit. Note the town's pretty *lavoir* (open-air laundry), beside the Rue des Argillières, using the clear waters of the Aunette river.

The ancient wars are long forgotten in the charming villages of **Saint-Germer-de-Fly**, with its 12th-century abbey church, and fortified **Gerberoy**, notable for its old houses of timbered red and yellow brick and their exquisite little gardens.

South of Rouen

The heights of **Les Andelys** command a wonderful view of the Seine river and valley from the fortress of **Château Gaillard,** built by Richard the Lion-Heart in 1197 to stop his old ally Philippe Auguste from approaching Rouen. It was Philippe's conquest of this fortress by siege (and a final assault up through the latrines) that ended the duchy's independence from the French crown. The chalk cliffs that you see to the north-west were once interspersed with slopes of vineyards, before wine was gradually edged out by cider.

Giverny is famous as the home of Claude Monet, which has been lavishly restored with brand new furnishings, artefacts from his studio and the collection of Japanese prints that provided some of his

inspiration. His paintings are presented only in ingeniously deceptive photographic reproduction. The main attraction is the beautiful garden, complete with the Japanese bridge, water lilies and rose bowers that were among the Impressionist master's favourite subjects.

In attractive hilly surroundings south of the Seine's tributary, the Eure, the proud old cathedral city of **Evreux** was bombed first by the Germans in 1940, then by the Allies in 1944,

but has made an impressive revival.

Start out at the miraculously preserved **Tour de l'Horloge,** an imposing 15th-century clock tower opposite the town hall, and take the **lovers' promenade** along the remains of the city ramparts that follow the jolly little Iton river.

The **Cathédrale Notre-Dame** was built on the site of a Roman basilica (at which time the town was known as Mediolanum Aulercorum). Most of

Henri IV left the Château Gaillard in ruins rather than let a potential enemy use it against him.

the church is Gothic, from the 13th to the 16th century, when the airy Flamboyant north porch and transept were added. But inside, the nave's great Romanesque arches have survived centuries of fires, the pillar capitals adorned with the characteristic Norman sculpting of flutes, curves and interlaced **39** tracery rather than human figures or animals. In the ambulatory around the choir, note the Renaissance carving on the chapels' wooden screens.

The treasure of the old abbey church of **Saint-Taurin** is the exquisite 13th-century **reliquary**, designed like a miniature cathedral of gold, silver and enamel with rubies and other precious stones, its delicate statuary depicting the legendary life of Saint Taurin, first Bishop of Evreux.

Route des Abbayes

The D982 highway leading west from Rouen on the north bank of the Seine is the beginning of the well-signposted "Route des Abbayes" that winds through woodland and meadows around the abbeys that organized Christianity in Normandy from the 7th and 8th

Since 1948, Benedictine monks are back at Le Bec Hellouin abbey, but their refectory is now the church.

century on. After being sacked and plundered continuously by the Norsemen, the abbeys enjoyed a new heyday under the Norsemen's most illustrious descendant, William the Conqueror.

Twelve kilometres (8 mi.) from Rouen is **Saint-Martin-de-Boscherville,** site of the 12th-century **Eglise Saint-Georges**—one of the few abbey churches not to have served as a stone quarry for masons during or after the Revolution. (It was converted for use as the parish church.) There are both strength and quiet harmony in this masterful late Romanesque building. Inside, the sculpture on the capitals is mostly geometric or floral, but varied with a series of mythic monsters, the abbot blessing his flock and a couple of battling knights on horseback.

Of all the abbeys, the grandiose ruins of **Jumièges** occupy a special, romantic place. For a superb view, drive through the

Forêt de Brotonne along the D313 south of the Seine and then take the ferry across the river at Port-Jumièges.

The white granite shells of the abbey's two churches, the Romanesque **Notre-Dame** and smaller Gothic **Saint-Pierre**, with trees and grass growing in and around the nave and chancel, survive their troubled end with moving dignity.

Duke William returned from his conquest of England to attend the consecration of Notre-Dame in 1067. Seven centuries later, the Benedictine monastery was disbanded during the Revolution, and the buildings were later blown up with explosives by a local merchant who had bought them cut-price in an auction. But the sturdy edifices resisted total destruction, and Notre-Dame's two soaring square towers (minus their original spires) dominate the remains.

A short drive north on the D982, **Saint-Wandrille**, founded in 649, is an active Benedictine monastery. Giving a modern twist to the venerable monastic occupation of copying illuminated scriptures, one of the major activities is putting sacred manuscripts on microfilm. The Gothic **cloister** and 17th- and 18th-century monks' quarters still stand, but

of the original 13th-century abbey church, only the northern transept survived the quarrying of the Revolution. It's been replaced by another 13th-century building, a timbered barn transferred by the monks, piece by piece, from a farm 50 kilometres (30 mi.) away and, with a new roof, consecrated as a church just in time for Christmas, 1969.

Completing this group of abbeys (but a little off the main route, some 30 kilometres [19 mi.] south-east of Pont-Audemer, off the D130), **le Bec-Hellouin** is one of the most picturesque of the ruins, in the lovely wooded setting of the Bec valley.

As you learn from a plaque on the **Tour Saint-Nicolas** (practically all that remains of the abbey church), this major centre of medieval learning was a veritable training school for the top jobs in the English Church, providing abbots for Westminster, Colchester and Ely, two bishops for Rochester and three archbishops for Canterbury.

South of the old church's remains is the Classical 17th-century palace-like **cloister**. In the new church are some 15th-century sculptures of the founding fathers, Ambrose, Augustine, Gregory and Jerome.

The Channel Coast

Popular "gateway" to Normandy for those crossing the English Channel from Newhaven, Dieppe is the principal seaside resort. From there, the white chalk cliffs of the Côte d'Albâtre (Alabaster Coast) run west to the great industrial port city of Le Havre. Behind the coast are the beech forests and dairy farms of the broad, rolling Pays de Caux.

Beginning at the fishing and sailing port of Honfleur, the Côte Fleurie (Floral Coast) embraces a series of elegant family resorts of which Deauville is the most celebrated. The Côte du Calvados (Calvados Coast) includes the beaches of the D-Day landings, behind which lie the historic cities of Bayeux and Caen.

In Deauville, a daily walk along the planches *is almost obligatory.*

Dieppe

The **harbour** conjures up, in miniature, something of the bustle of the grand ocean ports in the heyday of transatlantic liners and sea trade with exotic lands. Holiday-makers at the **Avant-port** (ferry port) do without baggage-porters or drive their own cars off the boat. Across the Pont Colbert drawbridge, almost a horizontal version of its contemporary, the Eiffel Tower (1889), is the Bassin Duquesne fishing port. The nearby early-morning **fish market** for scallops, sole, turbot and sea bass is about as lively as the phlegmatic Dieppois fishermen ever get. At the **Bassin de Paris**, in place of the old freighters from Guinea that brought elephant tusks and whales' teeth for Dieppe's time-honoured ivory-carvers, you'll find colourful banana boats from Morocco.

The pebble **beach**, very fashionable in the 19th century, is more popular these days for stretching your legs than for bathing, with a good view west to the Ailly lighthouse.

The 15th-century **Château de Dieppe** (Rue de Chastes), built to defend the port against the English after they were driven out in the Hundred Years' War, is now a museum devoted

to the town's venerable seafaring traditions. Among its collection of model sailing ships is *La Dauphine*, in which Giovanni da Verrazzano sailed from Dieppe to discover the bay of what he proposed calling Land of Angouleme but is now known as New York. Pride of place goes to the intricate scrimshaw carving in ivory—compass boxes, sewing caskets and ships in bottles dating from the 18th century, but also fine 19th-century work by Pierre Graillon who raised the craft to the art of sculpture. Look, too, for the comprehensive collection of engravings by Cubist Georges Braque.

The courageous but abortive Canadian raid on Dieppe in World War II is commemorated in the **Musée de la Guerre et du Raid du 19 août 1942** (2 km. [about a mile] west of town on the D75). Built at the radar station that was one of the raid's main targets, the museum also exhibits Allied and German tanks and the deadly V-1 rockets loaded with explosives that were fired across the Channel from German air bases in Normandy in 1944.

Just west of Dieppe, on a grassy hedgerowed plateau overlooking the sea, the tranquil, rustic resort of **Varengeville-sur-Mer** offers bracing cliff-top rambles as alternatives to the sea-bathing at nearby Pourville and Quiberville.

The **Parc des Moustiers** is a year-round delight, famous for its giant rhododendrons and azaleas blooming from April to June, for roses and hydrangeas in July and August, and for the autumn foliage of its exotic trees from China, Japan and the Americas. In the middle of the park is a 19th-century **mansion** designed in the style of the English Arts and Crafts movement by Edwin Lutyens, architect of imperial New Delhi. Take a peek inside at the furniture and Pre-Raphaelite décor that includes a Burne-Jones tapestry.

A house of another age is the **Manoir d'Ango** (south of town, off the D75). The grand 16th-century residence was built for Dieppe's greatest shipping magnate, Jean Ango, by Italian Renaissance architects and sculptors. The spacious arcaded courtyard is dominated by the ornate dovecote of the main lodge, subtly combining brick, flint and sandstone. Ango made his fortune by rounding up pirates in the Mediterranean and sharing their spoils with King François I, a guest of this manor.

In the village **church** is a stained-glass window by Georges Braque, who spent his last days at Varengeville and is buried in the church cemetery.

Pays de Caux

North-east of Dieppe, **Le Tré-port** is a popular day-trippers' resort with something of the happy-go-lucky atmosphere of the English seaside.

A short drive inland, off the D126, the **Forêt d'Eu**, with its beautiful groves of beeches and oaks, is ideal for hiking along clearly marked paths, one of them specially laid out for amateur botanists.

Somewhat larger than its name, the town of **Eu** has

Despite the industrialization of Normandy's agribusiness, some of it is still done by hand.

a fine 13th-century Gothic church, **Eglise Notre-Dame et Saint-Laurent**, with a bright buff-stone interior. Look out for the 18th-century wooden *banc d'œuvre* (churchwarden's pew), bizarrely ornamented with four cannons on its canopy—it was offered to the church by Louis XIV's Master of Artillery, the Duke of Maine.

Arques-la-Bataille, site of Henri IV's victory over the Catholic League in 1589, has an imposing ruined castle perched on the crest of a hill, an excellent example of feudal fortification. Built in 1040 by the uncle of William the Conqueror, it was the last fortress in the duchy to fall to the King of France in 1204 and resisted all English attacks in the Hundred Years' War. Its impregnability enabled Henri IV to defeat an army of 30,000 Catholics with only 7,000 royal troops. But it was less successful against the quarrying of 19th-century building merchants and bombardment in World War II.

Fécamp

To appreciate the panorama across the cliffs to the harbour with the old abbey church dominating the town behind it, leave the main highway to approach the town along the D79 coast road via SENNEVILLE. The best view is from beside the small roadside chapel of Notre-Dame-du-Salut.

The considerable Renaissance and Baroque reconstruction from the 16th to the 18th century and the iconoclasm of the Revolution have not overwhelmed the massive Gothic structure of the 13th-century **Eglise de la Trinité**. Since 1748, a Classical façade has replaced two towers at the church's western end, and the remaining bell tower now has a pyramidal roof in place of its spire, but the overall effect is still powerful. The most rewarding of its additions is the chancel's 15th-century Flamboyant Gothic **Chapelle de la Vierge** at the south-eastern corner—the main entrance.

But it's the interior that is most impressive. Take in the vaulted nave 127 metres (417 ft.) long—just 3 metres (10 ft.) shorter than Paris's Notre-Dame—from the rostrum at its west end. The Gothic sculp-

---

Strong Medicine

In 1510, Brother Vincelli went gathering wild hyssop, melissa and angelica on the Fécamp cliffs and distilled them with a few exotic oriental spices to produce a miraculous health elixir. The recipe was lost when the monastery was disbanded in the Revolution. In 1863, an enterprising entrepreneur rediscovered it among some old family papers, called the drink Bénédictine and made it a popular after-dinner tipple —with claims to health-giving properties.

tural group immediately facing the entrance is the 15th-century *Dormition de la Vierge*, the Sleeping Virgin surrounded by the Apostles. The Classical 18th-century choir culminates in a grandiose late Baroque gilded high altar and, beyond it, the more subdued white marble Renaissance altar of Italian sculptor Girolamo Viscardo. In the north arm of the transept are some superb fragments of the 15th-century choir screen, late Gothic sculptures of the Apostles at prayer.

In an almost hilariously ugly neo-Renaissance-cum-neo-Gothic building, the **Musée de la Bénédictine** (110 Rue

Alexandre-le-Grand) is devoted to the distillery of the famous liqueur and some art works salvaged from Fécamp's Benedictine monastery.

The bizarre formations of Etretat's cliffs have inspired painters, poets and picnickers.

Etretat

This quiet little resort has long been famous for the spectacular forms of the cliffs that frame its **beach**—on which the white marble-like pebbles are for once smooth enough to fall asleep on. (Local confectioners make sweets, *galets*, in imitation of the pebbles.)

The beautiful effects of erosion on the chalk cliffs have attracted to Etretat some of France's most illustrious artists and writers. Monet was fascinated by the delicate play of light on the sea and rocks, as were Courbet and Boudin before him and, later, Dufy, Matisse and Braque. Maupassant spent his childhood here and featured Etretat in his stories. The town was equally prominent in the adventures of that most sophisticated rascal of the Belle Epoque, gentleman-burglar Arsène Lupin, created by Maurice Leblanc.

For a close-up of the **Falaise d'Aval** (Downstream Cliff), take the enjoyable cliff-top walk, 60 minutes there and back, from a stairway at the south end of the beach promenade. There are three formations: the slender "Gothic" arch of the Porte d'Aval jutting out from the cliff; offshore, the sharply pointed 70-metre-high (230-ft.) Aiguille (Needle), **49**

which the Germans painted black during World War II; and, further south, the massive, more Romanesque arch of the 90-metre-high (295-ft.) Manneporte (Magna Porta or Great Gate).

The **Falaise d'Amont** (Upstream Cliff), at the north end of town, is also worth a trip

Honfleur has been the tranquil starting point of a thousand adventures on the high seas.

for the cliff-top walk and view back to Etretat from the Chapel of Notre-Dame-de-la-Garde (drive to the Avenue Damilaville, then 45 minutes' walk there and back).

cultural centre in concrete, the **Espace Oscar Niemeyer**, named after its Brazilian architect.

Another striking edifice is the glass, aluminium and steel **Musée des Beaux-Arts André Malraux** (Boulevard J.-F.-Kennedy) overlooking the sea. In addition to a good collection of European masters (Giordano, Ribera and Terbrueggen), the museum offers a great opportunity to see in one place the impact of Normandy on French painters: Boudin's pictures of Deauville, Trouville and Etretat; Monet's *Falaises à Varengeville*, Pissarro's *Bateaux à Honfleur* and Dufy's pictures of horse-racing at Deauville and scenes of Le Havre.

Honfleur

This pretty port has witnessed the beginning of nearly all Normandy's great seafaring adventures—and is still a mecca for sailing-enthusiasts.

Towering over the sheltered yachting harbour of the **Vieux Bassin**, the tall slate- and timber-façaded houses gleam in the sun or, even more striking, glisten in a thunderstorm. The perfect place to dream of the arrival of the first Norsemen and the departure of their grandsons on voyages around the world.

Le Havre

This industrial port city, second in the country only to Marseille, was devastated by Allied bombs during World War II, and the modern reconstruction makes an overwhelmingly rectangular impression. A notable exception, on the Rue de Paris, is the dramatic

Itchy Feet

Conquest and exploration, often amazingly far from home, were always a useful safety valve for the Normans' natural aggressive energies: England and Sicily in the 11th century, Sierra Leone in 1364, Brazil in 1503, Canada in 1506, Florida in 1563. Chicagoans to this day honour the passage of a great Rouen sailor who set out from Honfleur: the financial district of the Middle West's "Wall Street" bears the name of La Salle, who passed that way on his exploration of Lake Michigan and the Mississippi River in 1682.

Explore, too, the old shipbuilders' quarter along the **Rue Haute** running north-west from the **Lieutenance**, 16th-century remains of the royal governor's house at the harbour mouth.

The **Musée Eugène-Boudin** (Place Erik-Satie) is devoted principally to the work, some 70 pictures in all, of Boudin, who was born in Honfleur. His colourful studies of beach scenes and seascapes inspired the Impressionists, most notably Monet. The latter is represented by two important works, *La Plage d'Etretat* and *Le Clocher de Sainte-Catherine*. To learn more of the history of Honfleur's port, its pirate ships, slave trade and fishing, visit the **Musée du Vieux-Honfleur** (Quai Saint-Etienne).

A pleasant day-trip southeast along the D180, **Pont-Audemer**, like any town with two or three canals and a couple of humpbacked bridges in its centre, is inevitably known as some kind of "Venice". The canals of this agreeable little "Venice of Normandy" link two arms of the Risle river and flow past some attractive old timbered houses, notably on Rue Place de la Ville and Rue Sadi Carnot.

Côte Fleurie

Between the estuaries of the Touques and Dives rivers, the coast's 20 kilometres (12 mi.) of sandy beaches, handsome villas and beautifully weatherbeaten old hotels have great appeal for nostalgics of Napoleon III's Second Empire and the *Belle Epoque* of the 1900s.

Cleverly blending old-fashioned elegance with modern comforts, **Deauville** is the most prosperous of Normandy's seaside resorts—and also the most expensive. But even if your budget doesn't extend to one of those seafront *palaces*, as the French call their luxury hotels, stop off on the wooden promenade of the celebrated **planches** for some of the most amusing people-watching in France. This is where a company director takes his secretary for weekend business conferences and runs into his wife with the chairman of the board. The white sandy **beach** with its colourful canvas sun-shelters is a delight and the swimming perfectly good, but amazingly few people turn away from the spectacle on the *planches* long enough to go into the water.

Horse-lovers come for the summer racing, flat and steeple, and the prestigious yearling sale. What they win on the racing, they lose at the casino. The tennis and golf are first-class, but yachtsmen should bear in mind a Deauville proverb: If you can see the port of Le Havre, it will rain in the afternoon, and if you can't, it's already raining.

The oldest of this coast's resorts, **Trouville** (where the gentry used to send their domestics) is now a slightly downmarket Deauville. But it's just as lively, with an excellent beach, where people seem less frightened of swimming, and

Normandy menfolk don't mind doing the shopping for their wives' sumptuous cooking.

the bistrots on the port serve much better seafood.

The charm of **Houlgate** is in the trees and flowers of its gardens and the fine sands of its beach. Take the walk at low tide east to the cliffs of the Vaches Noires (Black Cows).

Cabourg is the most stately of the old resorts. Take tea at least at the **Grand Hôtel**, a true national shrine in which Marcel Proust wrote part of his *A la recherche du temps perdu*. It is the custom to fall asleep over

Old-fashioned grandeur at Cabourg, damp moments on Houlgate beach.

a leather-bound copy in your deckchair.

Across the river is the little town of DIVES-SUR-MER where, as they like to remind English visitors, William embarked in 1066. To rub it in, there's a Rue d'Hastings and a list of the Conqueror's companions on a wall of the parish church.

Caen

Apart from the remains of its historic centre, Caen's good hotels and excellent seafood restaurants make it, with Bayeux, a useful starting point for visits to the D-Day beaches. The first major objective of the Normandy landings, Caen took two months to capture and was devastated by Allied bombs and the shells of the Germans as they retreated.

Luckily, the noble silhouette of the **Abbaye-aux-Hommes** has survived. The church, **Eglise Saint-Etienne**, achieves a harmonious purity in the simple lines of the Romanesque towers crowned by their octagonal Gothic spires. Inside, once again complemented perfectly by the later Gothic architecture of the chancel, the **nave** is regarded as the finest example of Norman Romanesque still standing. Unusually lofty, its illumination is enhanced by the windows of the graceful lantern tower.

The first abbot, Lanfranc, became William the Conqueror's Archbishop of Canterbury. William, who had made Caen his Normandy home, founded the monastery, together with his wife Matilda's convent, Abbaye-aux-Dames, as a penitence following the granting of a papal dispensation for their marriage (they were cousins). The abbeys were paid for with the booty from his conquest of England. The elegant 18th-century monastery buildings now house the town hall.

Matilda's convent church, **Eglise de la Trinité**, is on the east side of town. The handsome towers of the western façade have lost their original spires, but the church, with the intricate rib-vaulting of its graceful nave, remains superb.

The remains of William's 11th-century castle boast an excellent collection of European painting in the **Musée des Beaux-Arts.** Highlights include Poussin's *La Mort d'Adonis*, Tiepolo's *Ecce Homo* and Rubens' *Abraham et Melchisédech*.

The nearby **Musée de Normandie** makes an interesting introduction to regional folklore and affords a better view of the castle itself, since World War II bombs destroyed the interven-**56** ing 19th-century buildings.

Bayeux

Proudly the first French town to be liberated in World War II, the day after D-Day, Bayeux was blessedly preserved from destruction. Its Gothic cathedral dominates a charming **old town** (*vieille ville*) of medieval and Renaissance houses on the Rue Saint-Martin, Rue Saint-Malo and Rue Bourbesneur.

But the town's most cherished treasure is the magnificent **Bayeux Tapestry** (or more correctly *embroidery*), created for Bayeux cathedral in 1077 to tell the story of Duke William's conquest of England. It is lovingly mounted in the Centre Guillaume-le-Conquérant (Rue de Nesmond) and accompanied by a fascinating film (in English and French) explaining the work's historic background.

No dry piece of obscure medieval decoration, the beautifully coloured tapestry gives a vivid and often humorous picture of life at William's court, with insights into medieval cooking, lovemaking and the careful preparations for war. These and the climactic Battle of Hastings are depicted with all the exciting action and violence of a modern adventure film.

Adding insult to injury, it was a group of defeated Anglo-

Saxon artisans who had to do the wool-on-linen embroidery (70 metres [230 ft.] long and 50 centimetres [20 inches] high), under the supervision of William's half-brother, Odon de Conteville, Bishop of Bayeux.

For those interested in the more recent history of the area, the **Musée Mémorial** (Boulevard Fabian-Ware) is one of the most impressive museums commemorating events from World War II. As well as an extensive exhibition of weapons and uniforms, the museum offers a comprehensive account of the Battle of Normandy.

Getting it in the Eye
The story told in the tapestry from the Norman point of view may come as a bit of a shock to the average Englishman. English King Harold is shown as a treacherous weakling who cheated noble, generous William out of the throne promised him by King Edward the Confessor (see p. 17). Scenes to watch out for: a unique view of the Mont-Saint-Michel without its later Gothic additions (panel 17); Halley's Comet flies over newly crowned Harold, a bad omen (panels 32–33); *Harold Rex Interfectus Est*—Harold gets it in the eye (panel 57).

D-Day Beaches

Until June 6, 1944, the peaceful stretch of coast west of Cabourg from Ouistreham to the Cotentin peninsula was known simply as the Côte du Calvados, a flat, undramatic shoreline broken by a few unspectacular chalk cliffs and sand dunes. Then, at 6.30 a.m., came the mighty fleet of Operation Overlord that turned the beaches into beachheads, with their now illustrious code names of Sword, Juno, Gold, Omaha and Utah.

Today, with the flames and dust of battle long gone, the coast has retrieved its calm. At a site so charged with the emotion of war and death, the atmosphere of rather bleak serenity is in itself as evocative as the few remaining hulks of the Allies' rusty tanks and boats, the Germans' concrete bunkers and blockhouses, some simple monuments on the sites of the action and the miles of crosses at the military cemeteries. (Caen and Bayeux tourist offices can direct you to the 27 Allied and German military cemeteries in the region.)

To see where the British and Canadians, with the support of the Free French forces, attacked on the eastern half of the beaches, start out at the port town of **Ouistreham-**

Riva-Bella. A museum (Place Alfred-Thomas, opposite the casino) details the combined Anglo-French operation to capture this stretch of Sword Beach, with uniforms and weapons used during the action. You can also visit the **Musée du Mur de l'Atlantique** (Avenue du 6 Juin), an authentic reconstruction of an artillery observation post on the Atlantic Wall.

Drive west along the D514 to BERNIÈRES and COURSEULLES, where the Canadians staged their Juno Beach landings, marked by monuments on the beaches and the Canadians' cemetery at Reviers.

At **Arromanches**, you can see the most fascinating monument to British ingenuity in the Allied landings—the remains of the artificial **Mulberry harbour** (best viewed from an observation post east of town). The steel and concrete jetties and pontoons, floated across the Channel, were the only way to unload tanks and heavy artillery on to a coastline (Gold Beach) without natural harbours. In town, the **Musée du Débarquement** on the seafront includes an exciting film explaining the whole heroic action.

The Americans' Omaha and Utah beaches, from Colleville

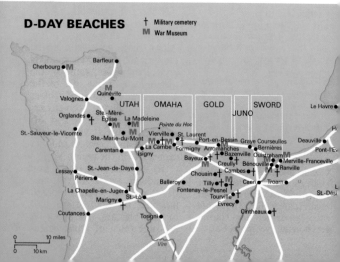

D-DAY BEACHES

† Military cemetery
M War Museum

Cherbourg • M
Barfleur •
Valognes • M Quinéville •
Orglandes † Ste.-Mère-Église
St.-Sauveur-le-Vicomte • La Madeleine
UTAH OMAHA GOLD SWORD
JUNO
Le Havre •
Ho
Ste.-Marie-du-Mont • Vierville • St. Laurent Port-en-Bessin • Graye Courseulles Deauville •
Pointe du Hoc M M Bazenville • Bernières Pont-l'Ev
Carentan • La Cambe Formigny Arromanches • Oustreham M
Isigny M Bayeux • Creully † Bénouville • Merville-Franceville
Lessay • St.-Jean-de-Daye • Tilly • Chouain Cambes † Ranville
Périers • Ballery • Fontenay-le-Pesnel Caen • Troarn •
La Chapelle-en-Juger † St.-Lô Tourville • Evrecy • L
Marigny • Torigni • Cintheaux † St.-Dési
Coutances •

0   10 miles
0   10 km

Vire
Orne

The Normans remember their Allied liberators with humour and affection.

to La Madeleine, are now official map references, a cartographer's tribute to the theatre of the fiercest fighting in the D-Day landings. The desolate coastline frequently recalls the stormy conditions that prevented the Americans from setting up their own Mulberry harbour to land their equipment. More eloquent than any museum are the 9,386 white marble crosses (and occasional Jewish Stars of David) of the **American military cemetery** overlooking Omaha Beach at COLLEVILLE-SAINT-LAURENT.

There are 21,160 tombs in the German military cemetery at LA CAMBE, on the N13, 7 kilometres (4 mi.) inland from Grandcamp-les-Bains.

You can see remnants of the battle for Omaha Beach on the **Pointe du Hoc** promontory, with its grassed-over bomb craters and shattered German bunkers. In one massive bunker, relatively intact, you can make out its mess room, dormitories, shooting-slots—and a bronze plaque to the U.S. Rangers who died taking the position.

The **Utah Beach** monument and **Musée du Débarquement** are at the base of the Cotentin peninsula, 5 kilometres (3 mi.) inland from La Madeleine, near SAINTE-MARIE-DU-MONT. A further museum at SAINTE-MÈRE-EGLISE (Place du 6 Juin) commemorates the airborne troops, with exhibitions of weaponry, uniforms and photographs.

The Mont-Saint-Michel and the Cotentin

No way around the claim of its most fervent admirers, the Mont-Saint-Michel island sanctuary, now joined to the mainland by a causeway, at the border between Normandy and Brittany, is indeed a *Merveille de l'Occident*—a "Wonder of the Western World".

It stands at the bottom of the Cotentin, within easy reach of tranquil beach resorts leading up the coast to the more rugged shoreline of the Nez de Jobourg, at the tip of the peninsula. Inland is the beginning of Normandy's *bocage* country that American troops had to fight for "hedge by hedge" from Utah Beach to Avranches —with bulldozer blades fixed to their tanks. The Abbaye de Hambye still stands in noble ruin, while the great Gothic cathedral of Coutances and Romanesque abbey church of Lessay have both recovered from the ravages of that 1944 Battle of Normandy.

☩ The Mont-Saint-Michel

Seeing for the first time the steepled abbey rising on its rock from the sea is a moment invested with ineffable mystery.

Whatever your faith or lack of it, sooner or later a visit to this formidable and exquisite fortress of the Christian Church is imperative.

Sooner or later, because you must choose your moment. If you want to recapture something of the atmosphere of the medieval pilgrimages, when thousands of the faithful swarmed across the island, loading up with souvenirs and fake relics and fighting their brethren for a meal or a bed, join the new secular pilgrims in the summer months, arriving by the busload rather than by mule. But if your mood is more contemplative, go in the early spring, autumn or even winter, when you can wander round the abbey and its village like a monk.

It's also worth planning with care your first view of the abbey—at a distance. Coming from Caen, you can stop in Avranches for a panorama of the bay from the Jardin des Plantes. Or drive out to the coast road (D911) between Saint-Jean-le-Thomas and Carolles. Best of all, if you're prepared to splash out and get high above the madding crowd, you can fly over the abbey on one of the special excursions organized from Avranches airport. Even if you have no time or any of these, do at least get off the main highway, the N176, when approaching the Mount to take the D43 coast road via Courtils for that all-important first glimpse.

The bay around the Mount's 80-metre-high (263-ft.) granite outcrop has been steadily silting up in recent years so that the abbey and its dependent village are a complete island only during the exceptionally high tides of the spring and autumn equinox. Then the sea comes in at a rate of nearly 50 metres (164 ft.) a minute over a distance of 15 kilometres (9 mi.). This proved very dangerous to the pilgrims who approached the abbey across the sands (the causeway was not built until 1874). Today, you can walk all around the Mount at low tide

One of those rare moments when a spring tide envelops the island of the Mont-Saint-Michel.

to see its various perspectives —and the beautiful patterns left in the sands by the flow of the Couesnon river. But first obtain reliable information about the tides so as not to end up stranded on a sandbank —or worse.

On what was once a Celtic burial ground (originally named Mont-Tombe) used as a refuge by a few Christian hermits, the bishop of nearby Avranches, Saint Aubert, began by building an oratory in 708 at the prompting, he said, of the Archangel Michael (a hill top being the traditional site of shrines dedicated to Saint Michael). In 1017, Benedictine monks started on the flat-roofed abbey that you can see in the Bayeux Tapestry (see p. 57), propped up on a platform with blocks of brown granite transported from the islands of Chausey, 40 kilometres (25 mi.) away.

The sanctuary was soon thriving with the offerings of thousands of pilgrims, including King Henry II of England and Louis VII. Wealthy Norman lords were persuaded to join the order and present their property to the abbey. By the 13th century, it had added new monastic buildings that together became known as the *Merveille* (Marvel) and was surrounded by a prosperous fortified village. The pilgrims continued to flock there during the Hundred Years' War, paying tolls to the English, who gov

Whose Abbey?

It is understandable that Brittany and Normandy should fight over the paternity and ownership of such a prestigious monument as the island-abbey of the Mont-Saint-Michel, at the frontier dividing the two provinces. The Bretons claim seniority. The Romans did lump the Cotentin peninsula together with Brittany as "Armorica" and, geographically, the rugged region is certainly part of the Armorican plateau, completely different from the greener hedgerowed meadows of the Normandy *bocage* to the east. Under the Franks, as part of the Avranches diocese in the *comté* (county) of Cotentin, it was handed over to Brittany in 867 by King Charles the Bald. But the Cotentin was ceded 70 years later to the newly founded Duchy of Normandy and has remained part of Normandy ever since.

Guide books don't like ruffling regional sensibilities and most of them—Berlitz included—have the venerable abbey in both books, *Brittany* and *Normandy*.

erned the surrounding territory but could never break through the mount's defences. After a steady decline under self-seeking, dissolute abbots, the monastery was dismantled even before the Revolution, but was saved from total destruction only by being converted into a state prison.

Beginning on the upper terrace with an extensive **view** of the bay, the hour-long guided tour (English, French or German) takes you through three levels of abbey buildings: the church, cloister and refectory at the top; the crypts, Knights' Hall and Guests' Hall in the middle; and an earlier sanctuary, a storeroom and almonry underneath.

The sturdy 11th-century Romanesque nave of the **abbey church** contrasts with the delicate lines of the Flamboyant Gothic chancel built in the 15th century. Note how the columns of the chancel's slender arcades soar on up to the elegant rib vaulting in a superb élan unbroken by intermediary bands or capitals. The transept and chancel stand not on the island's granite core but on a platform formed by three crypts, Notre-Dame-des-Trente-Cierges (Our Lady of the 30 Candles) to the north, Saint-Martin to the south and,

directly under the chancel, the massive columns of the **Crypte des Gros-Piliers**. Outside, climb up an elegant stone-traceried stairway to the double tier of the **flying buttresses** bracing the chancel. (Great view of the bay while you're up there.) The spire topped by a statue of Saint Michael is a 19th-century addition.

The **cloister**, with a staggered row of sculpted columns around the little garden, creates a perfect framework of grace and delicacy for a moment's meditation. In that magic space looking out to sea (through three large bays, now glazed, that were to lead to a never-built chapter room), the cloister is the crowning element of the *Merveille*. To the east is a spacious **refectory** with arched wood-panelled ceiling and subtle lighting through mere slits in the tall windows. Below are the brighter, imposing **Knights' Hall** *(Salle des Chevaliers)*, believed, in fact, to be the scriptorium, the monks' manuscript room; and the elegant **Guests' Hall** *(Salle des Hôtes)*, for V.I.P.s as opposed to the poorer pilgrims who were given shelter in the austere almonry in the basement.

On the same level is the appropriately named **Notre-Dame-Sous-Terre** (Our Lady

Beneath the Earth), a pre-Romanesque sanctuary of the 10th century, probably built on the site of Bishop Aubert's original oratory.

In the village, walk around the medieval **ramparts** and look out among the souvenir shops and cafés for the few surviving 15th- and 16th-century **houses**, notably the Lycorne spanning the street and the wood-framed Auberge de la Sirène.

Avranches

Avranches is situated at the mouth of the Sée river on the Baie du Mont-Saint-Michel. The diocese supervised the building of the first sanctuary and preserves in its **Musée de l'Avranchin** (Place de Saint-Jean-Avit), an exquisite collection of the abbey's illuminated manuscripts. Documents trace the life of the abbey from the 8th to the 15th century.

In the treasury of the otherwise unremarkable 19th-century **Eglise Saint-Gervais-et-Saint-Protais** is the skull of Saint Aubert, with a dent in it caused, it is said, by Archangel Michael prodding the hesitant bishop to build his sanctuary.

The arboretum of the **Jardin des Plantes** includes fine specimens of Japanese gingko and cedar of Lebanon. Behind the terrace, with its stunning view

of the Mont-Saint-Michel, is an 11th-century Romanesque porch surviving from the chapel of Saint-Georges.

Also overlooking the bay, the Square Becket, commonly known as **La Plate-forme**, marks the site of the old cathedral where Henry II did penance for the assassination of Archbishop Thomas à Becket.

But for anybody who lived through World War II, Avranches also marks the momentous entry into the Battle of Normandy of General George Patton. On August 1, 1944, he rolled into a town in almost total ruin at the head of a column of tanks that enabled American troops to effect the vital "breakout" from their arduous "Battle of the Hedgerows" across the *bocage* of the Cotentin. With the capture of Avranches, Patton could push on to liberate the Brittany ports and then turn around to drive the Germans back across the Rhine. These events are celebrated in the Musée de la Seconde Guerre Mondiale, near the **Patton Monument** at the south-east corner of town, beside the N175 leading to the Mont-Saint-Michel and the ports of Brittany.

The D911 coast road takes you to a couple of pretty resorts

Storing hay for the cold winters on a farm near Avranches.

on the bay. GENÊTS is the spot at which medieval pilgrims set off on a perilous 6-kilometre (4-mi.) journey across the sands to the Mount, hoping the tide would stay low till they got there. Be careful. There are a couple of safer hikes from CAROLLES: to the Cabane Vauban, an 18th-century cliff-top guardhouse, or down through the Lude valley to the sea.

Cotentin Interior

Why has the pretty little town of **Villedieu-les-Poêles** attached "frying pans" to its name? Because, as you'll see when you drive down the main street, that's its age-old glory: gleaming hand-made copperware. Over the centuries, the town converted from bells—for cathedrals from Normandy to Quebec—to frying pans, saucepans and kettles, nowadays coated inside with stainless steel or aluminium.

Visit the **museum** (Rue du Général-Huard) to see the fascinating range of copperware manufactured here since the 13th century. Villedieu was on the route for the copper being shipped from Spain to England.

The ruins of the great Romanesque-Gothic Benedictine **Abbaye de Hambye**, built in the 12th and 13th centuries, enjoy a magnificent setting in the wooded valley of the Sienne river. Besides the shell of the church, the surviving monastery buildings include a cider press, kitchen, stable and pigsty.

North-east of the abbey is the heart of the *bocage* country that bore the brunt of the 1944 "Battle of the Hedgerows". In the struggle, the historic city of SAINT-LÔ was almost totally destroyed, but the surrounding countryside has retrieved a wonderful serenity that you can admire from atop the **Roches de Ham** (south of Saint-Lô, just off the D551). A rocky ledge (with a very welcome little café nearby) provides a panoramic view over the farmland beyond steep cliffs and the dense forest of the Vire valley.

Roman capital of the Cotentin, **Coutances** boasts the superb Gothic **Cathédrale Notre-Dame**, with two characteristic Norman multiple-spired towers on the western façade. Inside, at the crossing of the nave and transept, note the elegant columns rising to the grandiose octagonal rib-vaulted dome of the lantern tower.

South of town, just outside SAUSSEY, look out for a country house signposted as an antique shop. Even if not antique-hunting, take a look at the lovely rose garden and a typical Normandy *gentilhommière* (gentleman's manor).

On the D244, north of the road to Coutainville, the **Château de Gratot** is a moated manor built in various stages from the 13th to the 17th century, hosting a popular arts festival in the summer. You can climb (carefully) around its nicely restored roofless lodge and four noble but dilapidated towers.

Cotentin Coast

Granville, a colourful fishing and sailing port, was created by the English in the 15th century as a stronghold from which to launch attacks on the Mont-Saint-Michel. Under the French, the town made most of its fortune from piracy, plus a little

Welcome break after a good catch of tourteaux and spider crabs

(long-gone) oyster-fishing on the side.

With hotels, casino, thalasso-therapy and commercial centre down below, the mansions in the fortified **Haute-Ville** of its 17th- and 18th-century heyday remain blessedly unspoiled. You'll find the best of them, built of Chausey Island granite, along the Rue Saint-Jean and Rue Notre-Dame.

Walk out to the west end of the promontory, to the **Pointe du Roc** for a view across to the Chausey Islands and the coast of Brittany. The nearby **aquarium** has an exotic collection of fish, seashells and coral.

For a cool swim or bracing old-fashioned walk along the promenade, **Coutainville** makes an attractive overnight stay. There's a sandy beach south of the jetty and smooth pebbles to the north.

The abbey church of **Lessay** is one of the great Romanesque monuments of Normandy, suffering terrible destruction in World War II but now beautifully restored. Built in the 11th century, it is one of the earliest churches to use rib vaulting to span a wide nave, heralding the technique that was to be one of the hallmarks of French Gothic architecture. It has the characteristic Benedictine plan in the form of a Latin cross with a finely proportioned, pyramid-roofed tower over the intersection of nave and transept. Extending from the western façade are graceful Classical buildings of the 18th-century abbey (no public access).

Barneville-Carteret is a quite lively resort, with water-sports facilities at the Barneville beach. And take the exhilarating **hikes** along the cliffs, the Sentier des Douaniers (Path of the Customs Men) down to the sea, around the rocky Cap de Carteret or over the nearby sand dunes of Hatainville.

Just south of the Cap de la Hague, where the Channel runs into the Atlantic, the rocky promontory of the **Nez de Jobourg** ("Jobourg's Nose") offers a dramatic seascape of steep cliffs and waves pounding on the rocks.

Most spectacular view of all is over the **Baie d'Ecalgrain** (along the D401 coast road). This was a popular spot for smugglers and pirates, while more sedate locals would patiently wait for the occasional shipwreck to deliver its treasure on to the beach.

Transit port for holiday-makers from southern England and vital bridgehead for the 1944 reconquest of Normandy, **Cherbourg** is too much of a bustle for a prolonged stay.

If you do have time to spare, the **Musée Thomas-Henry** (Rue Vastel) has two 15th-century Italian masterpieces—Fra Angelico's *La Conversion de Saint Augustin* and a *Pietà* attributed to Filippino Lippi—and some 30 romantic canvases of rural life in the Cotentin by Jean-François Millet.

The **Musée de la Guerre et de la Libération** (Fort du Roule) documents the invasion and liberation of the Cotentin peninsula and Cherbourg, with a fascinating range of memorabilia from the occupation years.

On the east coast of the peninsula, sleepy **Barfleur** is a favourite with the sailing fraternity. In the days when the English kings ruled over Normandy, Barfleur was a vital strategic harbour and as such was almost totally destroyed in the Hundred Years' War, subsequently suffering the steady erosion of the Atlantic. Traces of the medeval community survive in the square of the **Cour Sainte-Catherine,** but the town is mainly a creation of the 18th and 19th centuries.

Further down the coast at Quinéville is the **Musée de la Liberté** (Rue de la Plage), with exhibitions of photographs and videos giving a general overview of the war years.

Central Normandy

The *départements* of Calvados and Orne form the heart of Normandy. This is where the classical *bocage normand* comes into its own, with the hedgerows up on embankments surrounding clusters of houses that are more village than hamlet.

The region is within reach of resorts on the Channel Coast (see p. 52), which make good bases for explorations south to the Catholic pilgrimage town of Lisieux and the "cheese and apple" country of the Pays d'Auge—the gracious world of the gentleman farmer with his grand château-like manor house.

Crossing the hilly but scarcely mountainous Suisse Normande (Norman Switzerland) to the west, you come to the regional park of Normandie-Maine, which includes the fortified town of Domfront and the genteel hot springs resort of Bagnoles-de-l'Orne, as well as the hunting forest of Ecouves. Just north of the park lies the land of the stud farms. From another great hunting forest, the Perche, it is a short hop across the border of Normandy to the cathedral city of Chartres.

Lisieux

The industrial and commercial capital of the Pays d'Auge has become an immensely popular pilgrimage town since the 1925 canonization of Sainte Thérèse. A huge modern **basilica** has been built in her honour to receive the thousands of faithful.

Daughter of a wealthy and deeply religious family, Marie Françoise Thérèse Martin is said to have felt her vocation at the age of 9 and was granted permission by the Pope to enter the strict order of the Carmelites six years later. She was canonized not for any spectacularly saintly deeds or miracles, but for the exemplary dedicated purity and intense religiosity of her short life—she died at 24.

The 12th-century Gothic **Cathédrale Saint-Pierre** has a lofty simplicity appropriate to the town of Thérèse. The Flamboyant Gothic chapel added beyond the choir is the burial place of Pierre Cauchon, judge of Joan of Arc and, denied the Archbishopric of Rouen he coveted, Bishop of Lisieux (see p. 20).

Pays d'Auge

As the major centre for the production of cider and Calvados and the three great cheeses, Camembert, Livarot and Pont-l'Evêque, the Pays d'Auge is the epitome of rural Normandy in the popular imagination. Extending south from the Côte Fleurie of Deauville and Cabourg (see p. 52), it lies between the Touques and Dives rivers at the province's geographical centre.

If the vast agribusiness concerns of grain-growing eastern Normandy are the *nouveaux riches*, then the orchards and dairy farms represent the old duchy's landed gentry, typified by their gracious manor houses. And if there's not enough "old money" to keep the manors in shape, any number of Young Upwardly-mobile Professionals from Paris seem ready to invest in them as weekend and summer homes.

The **Route des Fromages** (Cheese Route) guides you around the tiny winding country roads past the farms and factories that produce the real thing. Cheese manufacture is mostly industrialized nowadays, but no less authentic, with careful quality control protecting Normandy's ancient pride. You can taste and buy from the *maîtres fromagers* (master cheese-makers). Addresses of approved farmers and manufacturers are available from the *syndicats d'initiative* at SAINT-PIERRE-SUR-DIVES, LIVAROT and Orbec.

The Pays d'Auge abounds in the raw materials of Normandy's prosperity: apples and cows.

Victim of all the wars and revolutions, but nicely restored, **Vimoutiers** is one of the main market towns for the best local cheeses. Monday has been market day ever since the monks of Jumièges started coming here in 1030 to sell the produce of their farms. Near the neo-Gothic village church is a modern statue of Marie Harel, to whom the locals attribute the invention of Camembert. The statue was donated by an American company from Van Wert, Ohio, manufacturing cheese alongside its electronics, steel and wood products. In the Viette valley, the village of CAMEMBERT itself is no more than a hamlet (off the D246, 4 km. [2½ mi.] south-west of Vimoutiers) with Marie Harel's Beaumoncel farmhouse still there.

Unlike the other big cheeses, Livarot restricts manufacture of its distinctively pungent product to the narrow confines of its own canton, in and around the villages of Boissey, VIEUX PONT (visit the Romanesque church, one of the oldest in Normandy) and Castillon. West of this canton, the major distribution centre of **Saint-Pierre-sur-Dives** holds its Monday market in splendid medieval Halles, three-aisled with massive timbered roof. You'll find a cheese museum in the grounds of the old abbey.

Though its cheeses, oldest of the Big Three, are produced along the "Route des Fromages", the town of PONT-L'EVÊQUE (north of the A13 *autoroute*) is outside the main region. On the Grande Rue Saint-Michel and Rue de Vaucelles, a few old houses of the 16th century have survived the wars.

There is also a **Route du Cidre**, signposted with a jolly apple on the arrow, but if you intend tasting along the way, try hiking or biking rather than driving. A circuit south-west of Pont-l'Evêque points out the **cider cellars** and ancient wood and granite presses that you can visit around the villages of CAMBREMER, BONNEBOSQ and BEAUFOUR. **Beuvron** has been kept spick and span as a model village of traditional timbered houses clustered round the old Halles.

Not signposted as such, but meriting your attention as you follow the cheese and cider routes, is an itinerary south of Lisieux around the great **manoirs** (manor houses) reigning in solitary splendour over the countryside of the Pays d'Auge. Enjoying their heyday from the 16th to 18th century, they range from handsome but

CAMEMBERT LE RÉGAL

PIERRE BARRÉ À LIEURY

par St Pierre %. Dives.
(Calvados)

DOMAINE DU MESNIL DE LIEURY

Where else but Normandy do you see little girls praying for cheese?

modest timbered farmhouses to veritable châteaux that add to the timber framework subtle and colourful combinations of stone, brick and slate, with all the turrets and fortifications needed in their troubled times. One of the grandest is the 16th-century **Saint-Germain-de-Livet**, built in Italian Renaissance style beside a tributary of the Touques river. Its turreted walls have a checkered pattern of sandstone and green-varnished bricks around a 73

courtyard with arcaded gallery. The 17th-century **Grandchamp** is another elegant combination of a brick and stone château joined on to a traditional timbered farmhouse. Other fine examples are the moated **Coupesarte**, still part of an active farm, **Bellou** amid its apple-orchards, and **Chiffretot**, with an imposing octagonal tower.

South-west of Chiffretot, just outside LISORES, the **Musée Fernand-Léger** has been created in a hillside barn on the 20th-century artist's family farm. The displayed works of this Cubist-turned-social-romantic include paintings, bronzes, mosaics and secular stained glass windows celebrating peasants and factory workers.

The gracious living that characterized the Pays d'Auge is summed up in the wonderfully preserved urban elegance of **Orbec**, with its Vieux-Manoir and other splendid Renaissance houses along the Rue Grande and Rue de Geôle.

Beuvron is a living museum of traditional timbered architecture.

Suisse Normande

Norman prudence is legendary. "Moderation in all things," they preach. So when they talk of Norman Switzerland, they don't need any Eiger, Matterhorn or Jungfrau. They make do, very prettily, with a couple of hilly plateaux in the Orne valley south of Caen, some fast-running streams for canoeing and fishing, gorges steep enough to tempt the climbers, and lots of cow pastures for picnics. Swiss enough?

The sheer cliffs of the **Roches d'Oëtre** (north-west of Putanges-Pont-Ecrépin) provide a dramatic view of the surrounding country. Behind the inn there (at the junction of the D301 and D329), you have free access to the tree-shaded ledge of rock. From 120 metres (394 ft.) up, there are three separate vantage points from which you can look out over the densely wooded gorges and meadows on either side of the meandering Rouvre river, a tributary of the Orne.

The village of **Clécy** is one of the region's most popular playgrounds, for adults and children. While the adults are playing with the miniature railway (nearly half a kilometre of tracks and 120 engines), the kids may have sneaked off to the cider cellars. Others are canoeing on the Orne, fishing for trout and pike in rubber waders from the middle of the ford beside the water mill, and picnicking, with a good view, up at the pine grove by the **Croix de la Faverie** south of town.

In this idyllic countryside, it comes as something of a shock to learn that villages like **Thury-Harcourt** were doomed to destruction in 1944—in this case because it was one of the Orne river's vital strategic bridge-heads. The 11th-century castle was burned in the bombardment, but stands in proud ruin in parkland along the water's edge. Leave your car, rent a

bike and take the delightful excursion north-west of town around the **Boucle du Hom** that follows a loop in the river.

Falaise

Lying east of the Suisse Normande, Falaise has two claims to fame, 900 years apart. It was here that Duke Robert was moved by the sight of Arlette, a local tanner's daughter, washing laundry at the fountain with her skirts drawn up to her thighs. He took her as his concubine and they had a son, William, who grew up as the Bastard and went down in history as the Conqueror (see p. 17).

In August of 1944, Falaise was a less romantic place. It became known to the world as a "pocket", a trap in which Canadian and Polish troops advancing from the north and Americans from the south were to encircle the German Seventh Army. With 90 per cent of the town destroyed by Allied bombing, the Germans broke out of Falaise, but the pocket closed around them further east, at Chambois.

On the square bearing his name, a ferocious 19th-century bronze **equestrian statue** of William rears, ready to charge, on a pedestal bearing the smaller figures of the first six dukes of Normandy. When you visit the nearby remains of the ducal **castle**, admire its massive proportions and grand position atop a precipice over the Ante valley, but ignore the guide's talk of a window from which Robert spotted Arlette or a room where William was born —the whole thing was built a century or two after William's death. In the castle chapel is a bronze memorial bearing 315 names of the *compagnons* who went with William to Hastings—British or American visitors may spot an ancestor among them.

North of the castle, commemorating the legend, is a modern Fontaine d'Arlette and behind it, next to the municipal swimming pool, a charming **lavoir** (open-air wash house).

The town's two main churches, **La Trinité**, near the castle, and **Saint-Gervais** (on the Caen road on the north side of town), are both largely Flamboyant Gothic and Renaissance in inspiration.

Normandie-Maine

This regional park covers a large area on the southern border of Normandy, spilling over into the region of the Loire Valley.

On the eastern edge of the park lies the medieval bastion of **Domfront.** From its strategic situation on a spur of rock 70 metres (230 ft.) above the Varenne river, it defended Normandy's south-western approaches, making it a major target in the 16th-century Wars of Religion and again, 400 years later, in the Battle of Normandy in World War II.

After Henri IV decided to dismantle the fortifications, only seven of the original 24 towers remained on the ramparts, and the ruins of the fortress are now part of a **municipal park** at the west end of the old town, with a view from the terrace over the Varenne valley.

Down by the Varenne river, as the church's name suggests, the 11th-century **Eglise Notre-Dame-sur-l'Eau** was an important station on the pilgrimage to the Mont-Saint-Michel. Despite having its aisles and four of the nave's six bays removed in 1836 to make way for a road to Mortain, it remains a gem of simple Romanesque architecture, with the transept and domed chancel reflected in the water.

Pears rather than apples dominate the orchards around Domfront, so try the local *poiré* (perry or pear cider).

Also in the park is the hot springs resort of **Bagnoles-de-l'Orne,** built around a little lake formed by the Vée river. Its 77

Quiet days on the stud farm before the yearling sales at Deauville.

balmy climate and low-mineral waters are recommended for insomnia and varicose veins. Other ailments can be treated by long walks in the nearby **Forêt des Andaines**. If that sounds too much like hard work, stroll among the chestnuts and oaks of the park— incorrigible lazybones take the miniature train—as far as the **Roc au Chien** for a panorama over the town and lake. Near the main spa building are a couple of rocks known as

the Saut du Capucin (Monk's Jump) in honour of a friar who jumped from one rock to the other after bathing in the waters.

In a region where the horse is still treated with particular reverence, the once royal stud farm of the **Haras du Pin** clings to three centuries of tradition with some 80 of the finest stallions in the country. They include Thoroughbreds, Arabs, Anglo-Arabs, French trotters and saddle-horses, sturdy Norman cobs and a dwindling stock of magnificent Percherons.

The Haras du Pin was completed under Louis XV and is justifiably known as the "Horse's Versailles" *(le Versailles du cheval)*. Drawing on their experience with the Palace of Versailles, Mansart designed the stud farm director's classical residence and red brick stables—laid out in the shape of a stirrup—and Le Nôtre drew up the plans for the grounds with characteristic geometrical avenues through the lawns and forest.

From February to July, the horses are farmed out to breed in the surrounding region. The rest of the year, you see them all here in their splendid stables, but even during those breeding months, a few are kept on the premises for special treatment and grooming. The best of the Thoroughbreds appear at the yearling sales in Deauville at the end of August.

Apart from the stable tour, there's a Thursday-afternoon parade of the horses in the summer, with coaches and all the traditional trappings of horsemanship. Showjumping and *dressage* competitions are held in the spring and summer. To see some of the offspring of these prize stallions grazing in the meadows, drive south-east of the Haras du Pin around the stud farms of the Merlereault region.

South-west of the Haras du Pin, the **Château d'O** is a fine mixture of Renaissance styles

The Way of All Flesh

Handsomest of all work-horses, aging from black to grey to gleaming white, the Percheron has been a steady victim of man's evolving technology.

Once, he was the favoured warhorse of the Crusader. In addition to the great strength that enabled him to carry the enormous weight of a knight in steel armour—the Percheron himself might weigh a ton—he had just the touch of Arab blood to make him fast enough to get his master out of trouble. With the advent of gunpowder and Napoleon's demands for ever speedier cavalry charges, just a humiliated few were needed for dragging artillery uphill. The rest went back to the farm.

Today, tractors and tanks have made him redundant, but still he is lovingly groomed at the Haras du Pin, three times a day, even though everybody knows his only destiny is horsemeat.

with Flamboyant Gothic details, a flourish of gabled roofs reflected in its pond. Take a quiet walk around the woods in the château's park.

After admiring in **Sées** the 13th-century stained-glass windows of the cathedral, visit the town's *syndicat d'initiative* for its excellent maps of the marked hiking paths in the nearby **Forêt d'Ecouves**.

Some of the paths cater to amateur botanists or tree-lovers in general interested in the wild flowers and particularly fine specimens of oak, beech and pine trees. It's also a great mushrooming forest—for experts who can recognize a *girolle* (chanterelle), *coulemelle* (parasol), *bolet* (boletus) or the ominously named, but perfectly edible and delicious *trompette de la mort* (craterellus).

The Signal d'Ecouves is marked on the maps as the highest point in Normandy, all of 417 metres (1,368 ft.), but it's

deep in the forest with no view of anything. More interesting —and incongruous—at the nearby Carrefour de la Croix-de-Médavy is the tank left stranded by General Leclerc's 2nd Armoured Division in 1944, now a monument to the French army contribution to the Battle of Normandy.

Surrounded by sleepy farms, the Château d'O is an island of Renaissance elegance.

The Perche

This south-eastern corner of Normandy, thick with forest and cattle farms, is popular hiking country for visitors coming into the province from Chartres (see p. 84). It rivals the Pays d'Auge for prosperous Parisians' weekend cottages and manors. In the Middle Ages, its pastures were the original breeding grounds of the Percheron horse.

Spick-and-span, the attractive hill-top town of **Mortagne**

lies at the heart of the region and commands a good view of the surrounding countryside. It's famous among gourmets for the quality of its *boudin noir* (black pudding)—try it fresh on the spot. Equally robust is the sturdy square-towered 16th-century **Eglise Notre-Dame**. The late Flamboyant Gothic church has an impressive Renaissance porch on the north side. Inside, stained-glass windows pay tribute to Mortagne's part in the colonization of Canada in the 17th century, when 150 local families settled in Quebec.

In the 2,000 hectares (nearly 5,000 acres) of the **Forêt du Perche** (and the contiguous Forêt de la Trappe), magnificent old oaks and beech trees cluster around a string of ponds formed by the Avre river—good both for fishing and a brisk swim. On the forest's western edge stands the abbey of the Grande Trappe (not usually open to visitors) where the Trappist monks still observe the strictest discipline of the Cistercian order, including the vow of silence.

South of the forest, **Autheuil** has a fine late 11th-century Romanesque church, notable for the lively sculpted capitals in the transept, with both human and vegetable motifs.

The region abounds in fortified farmhouses and castle-like manors, one of the most imposing being the stone-turreted **Courboyer** standing guard over the fields just north of the village of Nocé.

Finish your tour in the handsome town of **Bellême**. Stroll along the Rue de la Ville-Close

o admire the proud 17th- and 8th-century mansions, partic-ilarly numbers 24 and 26 and he Hotel de Ville and Palais e Justice.

In the nearby **forest,** the local tourist office organizes mushroom-picking led by specialists who can distinguish the edible from the poisonous.

The Perche country brings together hunting forests and the classical edgerows of the bocage.

Excursion to Chartres

Strictly speaking, it's not in the province, but Chartres is so tantalizingly close to the southeastern border that most Normandy holiday-makers can't resist a quick or even lingering side-trip.

It's one of the most moving experiences of a lifetime to drive through the wheat fields of the fertile Beauce plateau and see, looming suddenly on the horizon, the silhouette of **Chartres Cathedral**.

This unquestionable masterpiece of French civilization marks the transition in the 12th century from the solid, sober Romanesque style of the Church's beginnings to the more airy, assertive Gothic of its ascendancy. Apart from a few decapitated statues, it came remarkably unscathed through the Wars of Religion and the Revolution.

As you face the harmoniously asymmetrical western façade, the southern tower, **Clocher Vieux**, is a supreme expression of Romanesque simplicity, while the taller northern tower, **Clocher Neuf**, is already lighter, with its slender, more ornate steeple.

On the central porch, **Portail Royal**, note the stately, deliberately elongated sculptures of Old Testament figures, compared with the freer, more vigorous statues on the northern and southern porches.

Inside, the glory of the church is its **stained-glass windows**, with that unique "Chartres blue" and deep red, bringing an ethereal light into the nave, especially from a late afternoon sun through the western rose window, depicting the Last Judgment. Among the oldest and most famous of the windows, on the south side of the choir, is an enthroned Mary with Jesus on her lap, **Notre Dame de la Belle Verrière**.

The church is dedicated to Mary, representing her 175 times in the various sculpture and windows and paying tribute to her purity by admitting no tombs to its precincts.

In the paving of the nave's centre aisle, you'll notice a large circular **labyrinth** where, without chairs in medieval times, worshippers traced its path from the circumference to the centre as part of a mystic spiritual exercise.

Back outside, from the **Jardin de l'Evêché** (Episcopal Garden) at the rear of the cathedral, a stairway takes you down to the **old town,** with its streets of attractive 16th- and 17th-century houses along the Eure river—pretty view up at the cathedral.

What to Do

Sports

For all its many monuments and museums, Normandy cultivates an active outdoor life for sports-enthusiasts, energetic or merely spectator. The more elegant seaside resorts cater to the most fastidious shoppers, and gourmets will find their own kind of souvenir to take home. Traditional crafts are reviving, along with festivals secular and religious.

You'll find opportunities for most sports in Normandy, though you can safely leave your skis behind.

Jogging seems to have turned from fad to daily habit, marvellous through the forests or barefoot along the sands, and

From walking to water sports, you'll get plenty of exercise in Normandy.

even in town there's always a park or river bank where you can get away from the car fumes. Larger hotels increasingly have saunas and gyms to complete your work-out.

But to get the most out of the countryside, whether it be along the cliffs between Fécamp and Etretat or along the rivers and in the woodlands of the Suisse Normande, there's no better sport than **hiking**. Every little *syndicat d'initiative* can provide you with itineraries, many of them marked in red or blue on trees or lamp-posts along the trail. Near the great forests, some tourist offices propose guided tours for botany-buffs. Even for the most modest hike, be sure to equip yourself with proper footwear, not just skimpy tennis shoes. If you prefer **cycling**, you can usually rent a bike in the towns, very often at the railway station.

Nowhere in France is **horse-riding** more cherished than in Normandy—with 90 public riding stables throughout the region. You can rent a horse for the day at all the major coastal resorts, as well as at inland towns such as Lyons-la-Forêt, les Andelys, Clécy and Orbec.

Fishing is fine sport at the coastal resorts, whether angling from the shallows or out at sea in a rented boat. There are good trout and pike to be had in the inland ponds and streams, especially the fast-running tributaries of the Orne. Get your licence through the local *société de pêche* (fishing association).

Water sports are amply catered for. The Atlantic is, of course, much cooler than the Mediterranean for **swimming**. Be careful at some of the more secluded beaches where there

are no lifeguards on regular duty. Municipalities have excellent Olympic-size pools. The craze for **wind-surfing** has calmed down, but enthusiasts can still hire boards (*planches à voile*) at all the major resorts.

If you have to ask the price of a yacht, they say, you can't afford it. But **sailing** continues to grow in popularity. The major ports and resorts have first-class sailing schools. If price is no object, you can hire a 30-metre (100-ft.) vessel with ten-man crew at Honfleur or Dieppe. Inland, try **canoeing**, particularly in the Suisse Normande.

Back on dry land, possibilities for playing **tennis** are endless, so pack a racket. Tennis courts are mainly clay or hard court, in municipal parks or attached to hotels. The latter

Trotters make the pace at the summer races in Cabourg.

can often help you with temporary membership of private clubs. For **golf**, the best courses are at Deauville, Cabourg, Etretat, Dieppe and Granville.

Among the spectator sports, pride of place goes to **horse-racing**, most fashionable at Deauville, with yearling sales as well as races, culminating in the Grand Prix in the last week of August. But there's also a lot of fun at the smaller courses along the coast—Cabourg, Dieppe and Fécamp on the north coast and Coutainville and Grandville on the west coast of the Cotentin. Many of these resorts stage **showjumping** and **dressage** competitions, most spectacular at the Haras du Pin (see p. 78).

The **Tour de France** cycling race usually passes through Normandy in the early part of July. **Sailing regattas** take place throughout the summer, and a Tour de France yacht race sets off from the Normandy ports. Le Havre is the closest thing Normandy has to a first-class **football** team.

When the bottom fell out of church bells, Villedieu concentrated on pots, pans and bedwarmers.

Shopping

If you're not going into Paris before or after your Normandy trip, you'll find branches of most of the capital's smartest shops, particularly good for luxury silks, leather goods and jewellery, at Deauville.

At Honfleur, the ship chandlers around the Vieux Port have a tremendous range of sailing equipment, as well as all kinds of old brass paraphernalia, real and fake, from the town's golden age of buccaneers. In Dieppe, you can still find intricately carved ivory scrimshaw.

Bayeux is famous for its fine lace, white or black, in time-honoured floral designs. The town also boasts some of the most tasteful souvenirs in Normandy, taking advantage of the motifs from the ancient tapestry as decorations for table linen, mats, playing cards and wall hangings.

Hunters for antiques and second-hand books will find the best selection in Rouen. Rouen china is much prized (and highly priced), but you'll find attractive rustic pottery all over the province, particularly pitchers and mugs for cider. And the copper pots and pans of Villedieu-les-Poêles are without a doubt among the best kitchen utensils in the world. **89**

Gourmets who want to take a little of their gastronomic memories home with them should buy regional delicacies —the cheeses, sausages or pastries—at the end of the trip. In the drinks line, cider doesn't travel very well, but Calvados is a good investment—the older, the better.

Entertainment

Summer festivals of music— classical, jazz and rock—and other arts are held all over the region.

The Cotentin is very active. In May, you can attend the Coutances festival of Jazz Under the Apple Trees (*Jazz*

Festivals

In our increasingly sophisticated and blasé era, Normandy's calendar of folklore and religious festivals is dwindling, but they're still very colourful.

February/ March	Granville, *Mardi gras* (Shrove Tuesday) carnival with masked parades through the streets.
March	Mortagne-au-Perche, Black Pudding Festival.
Pentecost (7 weeks after Easter)	Honfleur, *Fête des Marins* (Sailors' Festival) at the port, with mass in front of Notre-Dame-de-Grâce. Pilgrimage to Lisieux.
Sunday closest to May 30	Rouen, procession and mass for Joan of Arc.
June 6	Utah Beach, D-Day memorial service at Sainte-Mère-Eglise, Sainte-Marie-du-Mont.
July 14	All over Normandy, Bastille Day fireworks and village dances.
July (last Sunday)	Granville, Maritime Guilds' torchlight procession, open-air mass.
September	*Foire de la Sainte Croix*, biggest fair in Normandy, 3 days of traditional cuisine, horse and dog market.
September (4th Sunday)	Lisieux, Sainte-Thérèse festival.
September (Sunday closest to 29)	The Mont-Saint-Michel, pilgrimage honouring the Archangel Michael.

sous les pommiers). The Mont-Saint-Michel organizes a series of chamber music recitals, *Heures Musicales*, throughout July and August, both in its own abbey and churches and in theatres at Avranches, Genêts, Granville and Lessay.

At Gratot (near Coutances) in August, there's a festival of modern ballet and theatre in the setting of its ruined château. The Château d'O near Sées holds open-air recitals in September.

Bayeux's July classical music concerts are performed in its cathedral. On the coast, Cabourg celebrates its most famous holiday-maker, Marcel Proust, with a June festival of romantic film, the answer to Deauville's festival of American film in September.

Seine-Maritime has its own summer arts festival scattered across the *département*, with events at Dieppe, Fécamp, Le Havre and Rouen.

Most of the coastal resorts have casinos, with Deauville claiming the grandest *Belle Epoque* décor. Formal dress is no longer required (though it should be "correct"). While you're playing roulette, baccarat or blackjack, you can park the kids—or the parents —in the next-door disco, an apparently essential accessory these days for every casino.

Eating Out

Normandy is a feast. The problem is keeping it in manageable proportions. The good seafood and beef, luscious cream and legendary cheeses, and the cornucopia from the orchards make it difficult to know when to stop. Our more diet-conscious, weight-watching days have put a rein on the old tendency to overdo the rich cuisine, one domain where traditional Norman prudence went out of the window. But there's still a good time to be had out there in the *bocage.*

Where to Eat

In bigger towns, you can choose between relatively expensive gourmet restaurants, large, family-style *brasseries* or more intimate little *bistrots*— both more moderately priced —and cafés for a cheaper snack. And even tradition-conscious Normandy has fast-food chains. The fixed-price *menu* (appetizer, main course and dessert) is very often the best deal, particularly in the major gourmet establishments where you get a first-class introduction to the restaurant's specialities without paying the higher *à la carte* prices.

Breakfast

In that lovely insular phrase which even the Americans seem to have adopted, the typical "continental" breakfast is still croissant, brioche or bread and butter with a jug of coffee, pot of tea or cup of chocolate. Increasingly, orange juice is offered as an extra, but you must insist on *orange pressée* if you want it freshly squeezed. Hotels offer English- and American-style breakfasts. But in town, we recommend you go out as often as possible to a corner café—it's great to watch a town getting up in the morning when you don't have to go off to work.

Lunch

Traditionally, a French lunch is as important as dinner, but you may not want to handle two big meals a day when you're travelling. A good alternative is a café salad or cheese, ham or pâté sandwich in long *baguette* bread or sliced *pain de campagne*. Or else a picnic. If you don't feel like shopping around a street market, *charcuteries* or *traiteurs* (caterers) pack complete meals, hot or cold, for you to take off to the country or a park bench. A corkscrew is more important than a credit card—don't leave home without it.

Dinner

The evening meal is usually served around 8 or 8.30 p.m., a little later in some of the seaside resorts. The French are much more relaxed than you might have expected about how you dress for dinner, and if the smarter places expect a jacket only a very few insist on a tie.

What to Eat

Before getting into Normandy's regional cuisine, it's worth noting some general French eating habits. First things first. Forgoing the starter *(entrée)* does not necessarily mean that the main course will be served more quickly. Besides, it's worth trying some of the simplest dishes that do work genuinely as appetizers: *crudités*—a plate of raw vegetables, green pepper, tomatoes, carrots, celery, cucumber, or just radishes by themselves served with salt and butter; *charcuterie*—various kinds of sausage and other cold meats, notably the *rosette* sausage from Lyon, the *rillettes* (a kind of soft pâté of pork or goose meat) and ham *(jambon)*; on a cold day, soups—fish *(soupe de poisson)* or vegetable *(potage)* most often with a base of leek and potato.

But in Normandy, it's a good idea to start with the fish

course. Trout *(truite)* is delicious *au bleu* (poached absolutely fresh), *meunière* (sautéed in butter) or *aux amandes* (sautéed with almonds). At their best, *quenelles de brochet* (dumplings of minced pike) are much lighter and airier than their English translation would suggest. Sole and turbot take on a new meaning when served with a *sauce hollandaise*, that miraculous blend of egg yolks, butter and lemon juice.

For your main dish, expect the meat to be less well-done than in most countries—extra-rare is *bleu*, rare *saignant*, medium *à point*, and well-done *bien cuit* (and frowned upon). Steaks (*entrecôtes* or *tournedos*) are often served with a wine sauce (*marchand de vin* or *bordelaise*), with shallots

What's your choice to accompany that giant tray of seafood?

(échalotes), or—rich sin—with bone marrow (à la moelle). Roast leg of lamb (gigot d'agneau) is served pink (rose) unless you specify otherwise.

And try some other regional cheeses as a comparison—and change—from Normandy's: blue Roquefort, the white-skinned Brie or the dozens of different goat cheeses (chèvre).

Desserts are the most personal choice of the meal, the moment you plunge back into childhood: in search of chocolate—a heavenly mousse au chocolat or diabolical profiteroles, little ball-shaped éclairs filled with vanilla ice-cream and covered with hot chocolate sauce; sherbet (sorbet)—blackcurrant (cassis), raspberry (framboise) or pear (poire); tarts and pies—apricot (abricot) or strawberry (fraise) and most magical of all, the tarte Tatin—hot caramelized apples, attributed to the Tatin sisters of Sologne after one of them accidentally dropped the tart upside down on the hotplate when taking it out of the oven.

Normandy's Specialities

It'll come as no surprise that the three basic elements of Normandy cuisine are the cow, the apple and the sea. Very little sign of garlic, and if olive oil is allowed into a salad, it's well concealed under the apple vinegar. Cream, butter, cider and Calvados pop up in every sauce, but no longer heavy with flour or other "foreign" thickener.

The classic sole normande is an elaborate concoction in cider and cream sauce with mushrooms, mussels, prawn or other shellfish. Canard à la rouennaise is a duck of unusually deep red meat served in a spicy sauce of red wine, its own blood and minced liver. The summit of regional self indulgence is achieved with the bonhomme normand (literally "Norman fellow")—a roast duck flambéed in Calvados, glazed with cider, all in a cream sauce decorated with a few slices of sautéed apples in case you forgot where you are.

Partridge (perdreau) and other game may be served in the same way. Succulent goose is more often braised (oie en daube). Rabbit is a much prized delicacy, making a savoury pâté and a main dish with morel mushrooms (lapin aux morilles) or stuffed with pig's trotters and truffles à la havraise (a speciality of Le Havre).

Robust eaters might like to know that tripes à la mode de Caen contain all the various compartments of the ox stom ach, along with the feet, plus onions, carrots, leeks, simmered all day or all night in a bouillon with cider and Calvados.

Tripe is so highly regarded in Normandy that since 1952, Caen's august fraternity of the Tripière d'Or (Golden Tripe Pot) awards an annual prize to the best tripe-cook. But Caen has a host of rivals: in the Perche it's cooked in layers, salted with bacon; in Coutances, prepared in little roulades of *gras-double* (ox stomach-lining) and cooked in cream; at La Ferté-Macé (near Bagnoles-de-l'Orne) skewered on brochettes —the centrepiece of an annual tripe fair at the end of April. Connoisseurs insist that good Normandy tripe should be eaten before 10 o'clock in the morning.

But the Normans' fascination with the ingenious things they can concoct with their animals' innards doesn't end with tripe. The pungent *boudin noir* (black pudding) is an intestine stuffed with a blend of pig's blood, fat and a subtle seasoning of herbs. In Normandy, most particularly in Mortagne, where it's a great speciality, the mixture is cunningly—inevitably—sweetened by finely chopped apples. It appears on menus with *pommes en l'air et*

Apples and pears offer some remarkably spirited possibilities.

pommes de terre (apple purée and mashed potatoes).

Like tripe, *andouille* (chitterlings sausage) is the subject of the most solemn attention **95** to quality and authenticity. Together with Guéméné-sur-Scorff in Brittany, the Calvados town of Vire claims with its centuries-old recipe to make France's only genuine *andouille* and the label *Véritable andouille de Vire* is a registered trademark. Each 30-centimetre-long (12-inch) sausage is hand-made from pig's stomach and intestines, salted and marinated for several days before being smoked black in beechwood for up to two months, then strung up, boiled and served cold as an hors d'oeuvres.

The *andouillette* is half the size of an *andouille*, grilled or sautéed, often in breadcrumbs, and served hot. The best ones come from Bernay and Rouen. Their interests are protected and championed by the A.A.A.A. (Association amicale des amateurs d'authentiques andouillettes—Fellowship of Authentic Andouillette Lovers).

Another, much lighter, speciality is the Mont-Saint-Michel's famous *omelette de la Mère Poulard*. This was created by the personal cook of a now forgotten architect sent at the turn of the century to take charge of the Abbey's restoration. Its grand reputation seems simply to lie in a com-

bination of the superior quality of Normandy eggs, cream and butter whisked to a soufflé-like fluffiness and the appetite worked up by the wind-buffeted causeway you have to cross to get to the abbey.

Try, too, Dieppe's *marmite de poisson*. This worthy northern response to a Marseille *bouillabaisse* is a hotpot of locally caught sole, turbot and angler fish *(lotte)* cooked in white wine and cream with celery, leeks, onion and fennel and

Quiet lunch among Yuppies at Normandy's grandest seaside resort.

topped with a few mussels, prawns and scallops. While Barville is proud of its mussels *(moules)*, Honfleur claims to fish the best prawns *(crevettes)*.

Local desserts include *bourdelots* and *douillons*, respectively apples and pears baked in a crusty pastry. A rice pudding cooked in milk, sugar and cinnamon, known variously as *terrinée, teurgoule* or *bourregueule* ("face-stuffer"), is served with *fallue*, a long pancake-like brioche.

Drink

A Norman's wine is his cider, sparkling and wire-corked in a champagne-like bottle. The fermented apples (or pears as perry, *poiré*, around Domfront) come out golden or ruddy in colour, popularly believed to help against gout, rheumatism and indigestion. **97**

The best is the *cru de Cambremer*, in the region west of Lisieux, slightly more bitter than most and so more refreshing, lower in alcohol than most English equivalents. Don't be surprised if it changes from day to day, clouding up or clarifying—it's natural. Drink it cool but not ice-cold.

Calvados is made from cider left in barrels for 1 or 2 years before being distilled like Cognac or Armagnac. It'll be acrid if it hasn't aged 5 or 10 years, and the great ones may be as much as 50 years old. Like good wines, it has an *appellation contrôlée*, the best being Pays d'Auge, then Vallée de l'Orne, Calvados, Avranchin and Cotentin. It's drunk as the famous *trou normand* (literally "Norman hole"), a digestive between courses of a large meal. Carry on at the end with the coffee, *café-calva*, then a *rincette* to rinse your mouth, then what's supposed to be the last, the *gloria*, before you're kicked out the door with what's known as a *coup de pied au cul*.

But when you're ordering something from outside Normandy, remember that French wines have far fewer rules than you might think. If you happen to like red wine more than white, you can safely and acceptably order red with fish;

a cool Brouilly, Morgon or Chiroubles of the Beaujolais family goes well with both fish and meat. Dry Burgundy or Loire Valley whites are indeed exquisite with fish and you can drink Alsatian whites with everything, with impunity.

But if you want a few basic pointers about the classic wines, the Burgundy reds divide easily into two categories, those that can safely be drunk relatively young—the supple *Côte de Beaune* wines of Aloxe-Corton, Pommard and Volnay—and those that need to age a little, the full-bodied *Côte de Nuits* wines of Vougeot, Gevrey-Chambertin, and Chambolle-Musigny. The great Burgundy whites include Meursault and Puligny-Montrachet.

Bordeaux wines have four main regional divisions: Médoc, aromatic, mellow red with a slight edge to it; Graves, an easy-to-drink red, dry and vigorous like the Burgundies; Saint-Emilion, dark, strong and full-bodied; and the pale, golden Sauternes, sweet and fragrant, perfect with *foie gras*. The lesser Bordeaux can all be drunk a couple of years old, but good ones need at least five years.

The Loire Valley produces fine dry white wines, such as Vouvray and Sancerre, and robust reds like Bourgueil and Chinon. Of the Côtes du Rhône, the best known red is the fragrant, deep purple Châteauneuf-du-Pape, but look out, too, for the Gigondas and Hermitage, and, for lunchtime drinking, the Tavel rosé. The great white wines of Alsace are known after their grapes—Gewürztraminer, Riesling and Sylvaner.

As after-dinner alternatives to Calvados, remember Cognac or the mellower Armagnac, and the fruit brandies *(eau de vie)* made from pear, raspberry, plum or cherry. Or, for an upmarket alternative to cider, Champagne, described by the connoisseurs as *aimable, fin et élégant*—"friendly, refined and elegant".

A votre santé!

The Big Cheeses

The success and worldwide demand for Camembert has led inevitably to "industrial" production, but that's been true since 1880. The streamlining of traditional methods does not mean in France a boring, homogenized product.

It's still a painstaking process. Milk straight from the cow (pasteurized only for export) with rennet, from a calf's stomach, as a curdling agent, is heated at 30 °C (87 °F) for two hours. The curds are put in flat cylindrical moulds: 2.2 litres for 1 Camembert, drained for 6 hours, left overnight, coated with salt and left a further 24 hours. It's then put on wattle racks in a drying room for 10 days and occasionally turned to achieve a uniform coating of white mould for its "skin". It stays another 10 days in a maturing cellar to

take on that characteristic faint yellow hue and supple texture before being wrapped and boxed. A ripe Camembert should "give" to thumb-pressure, without the skin puncturing.

Whereas Camembert is made with cow's milk from all over Normandy, Livarot production is limited to the narrow area of its canton. It takes 5 litres to make one Livarot and is matured over a month (3 to 6 months before "industrialization"). The ruddy-skinned Livarot, encircled with straw, is still pungent but no longer takes the roof off your mouth.

The square-shaped aromatic Pont-l'Evêque is the oldest of the Big Three (originally known as Augelot dating back at least to the 13th century). Three litres of milk go into each cheese, ending up a little drier than the other two.

To Help You Order...

Could we have a table?
Do you have a set menu?

Pouvons-nous avoir une table?
Avez-vous un menu du jour?

I'd like a/an/some...

Je désire...

butter	**du beurre**	milk	**du lait**
bread	**du pain**	mineral water	**de l'eau minérale**
chips	**des frites**		
coffee	**un café**	salt	**sel**
fish	**du poisson**	sugar	**du sucre**
fruit	**un fruit**	tea	**du thé**
ice-cream	**une glace**	(iced water)	**de l'eau (glacée)**
meat	**de la viande**		
menu	**la carte**	wine	**du vin**

...and Read the Menu

agneau	lamb	**fruits de mer**	seafood
ail	garlic	**gigot**	leg
andouillette	tripe sausage	**haricots verts**	string beans
artichauts	artichokes	**jambon**	ham
asperges	asparagus	**médaillon**	tenderloin
bœuf	beef	**melon**	melon
canard	duck	**moules**	mussels
carottes	carrots	**moutarde**	mustard
cervelle	brain	**nouilles**	noodles
champignons	mushrooms	**oignons**	onions
chou	cabbage	**petits pois**	peas
chou-fleur	cauliflower	**poireaux**	leeks
concombre	cucumber	**pommes**	apples
côtelettes	chops, cutlets	**potage**	soup
crevettes	shrimps	**poulet**	chicken
endive	chicory (endive)	**raisin**	grapes
		riz	rice
épinards	spinach	**rognons**	kidneys
flageolets	beans	**saucisse/ saucisson**	sausage
foie	liver		
fraises	strawberries	**saumon**	salmon
framboises	raspberries	**thon**	tunny (tuna)
frites	chips (French fries)	**veau**	veal
		volaille	poultry

100

BLUEPRINT for a Perfect Trip

How to Get There

Because travel possibilities are so complex and varied, the information given below can only be general. For specific and up-to-date details, consult your travel agent.

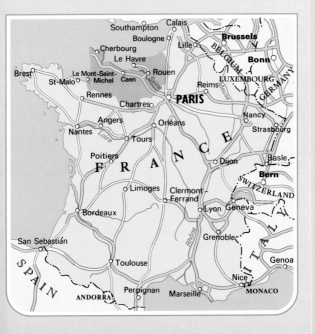

Most holiday-makers from the U.K. travel to Normandy by se
ferry, taking a car—and often caravan—for touring holidays. Oth
visitors, including those from the United States, Australia and Ne
Zealand, generally base themselves in London and cross from tl
southern Channel ports. To help cater for this, several tour operato
offer a taste of Normandy in the form of short-stay packages th
sometimes include a car.

BY SEA

Car and passenger ferries ply regularly throughout the year betwee
the southern English ports of Weymouth, Portsmouth and Newhave
and one or more of the main Normandy ports—Cherbourg, Le Havr
Dieppe and Ouistreham, the port for Caen. Crossing times vary fro
4 to 6 hours—depending on the route, tide and state of weather—ar
many overnight crossings are prolonged, enabling cabin passengers t
get a good night's sleep. There are direct sailings from Rosslare ar
Cork in the Irish Republic (the latter during the summer only), whic
take between 17 and 22 hours.

BY AIR

Regular flights operate from Gatwick to four of Normandy's six con
mercial airports—Caen, Le Havre and Rouen, with a summer servi
to Deauville. You can now fly to Rouen from Manchester. These fo
airports also have connections to other parts of France, including
regular service from Paris to Cherbourg and summer flights to Dea
ville from the French capital. You can reach Normandy by air fro
Brussels, Rotterdam and Düsseldorf (Le Havre) as well as Barcelor
(Rouen). There are also flights between the Channel Islands and Che
bourg, with a seasonal service to Granville and Deauville.

BY TRAIN

An efficient rail network from Paris enables you to reach most par
of Normandy easily. Paris's St-Lazare station serves the central ar
most coastal points, while trains from Montparnasse station cover tl
southern towns. The journey from St-Lazare to Dieppe, Le Havre c
Caen takes only about 2 hours, to Cherbourg less than 4. You can ge
to the south-western port of Granville from Montparnasse in aroun
3½ hours.

Anyone permanently resident outside France can buy the *Carte France-Vacances,* which gives unlimited travel for specified periods. Other offers by French Railways (SNCF) that apply to Normandy include: *Carte Couple/Famille,* issued free to married couples and families and allowing a 50 percent reduction on all journeys for one of the two adults and an additional 50 percent reduction on all children's fares; *Carte Jeune*, a seasonal offer of half-price for young people under 26, with a bonus of a free couchette; and *Carte Vermeil,* half-price rail travel for men aged 62 or over and for women of 60 or over.

But be careful: these offers don't apply to peak travel days. Ask at the railway station for a *Calendrier Voyageurs*, which shows by colour coding when you can begin each stage of your journey. Anyone can start travelling during "blue" periods, families also where it's marked white. Red indicates peak times, when you'll have to pay the difference.

When to Go

Many people consider that Normandy's climate, like its countryside, has more than a hint of southern England. You may encounter windy weather along the Cotentin peninsula, especially early and late in the year, although beaches on the west coast up from the Mont-Saint-Michel are more sheltered. Summer temperatures are generally pleasantly warm—never too hot—and there's less fog and mist than is encountered across the Channel. As for the rain, many a Norman will claim that it usually arrives at the same time as the ferries—a sure sign that the English can't do without it, wherever they are. Fortunately, there isn't too much evidence in summer to support that theory.

Here are some average temperatures for Normandy:

		J	F	M	A	M	J	J	A	S	O	N	D
Maximum	°F	47	47	51	54	59	64	67	67	65	60	53	49
	°C	8	8	10	12	15	18	19	19	18	15	12	9
Minimum	°F	40	39	41	45	49	54	57	57	56	51	46	42
	°C	4	4	5	7	9	12	14	14	13	10	8	5

*Minimum temperatures are measured just before sunrise, maximum temperatures in the afternoon.

Planning Your Budget

Prices vary considerably, particularly where hotels and restaurants are concerned. Here's a list showing some typical prices, with minimum maximum where relevant. They must, however, only be regarded a approximate, as inflation is ever present.

Baby-sitters. 30–40 F an hour, 150 F per day/evening, 300 F a week (beach club).

Bicycle hire. 50 F per day, deposit up to 500 F.

Camping. *Two-star* site inland: 2 adults, 2 children over seven (under seven free), car, caravan, electricity, local tax: 70–100 F a day.

Car hire (international company, taxes included). *Peugeot 309* 268 F per day, 3.88 F per km, 3,160 F per week (unlimited mileage). *Renault 21* 365 F per day, 4.85 F per km, 4,440 F per week (unlimited mileage).

Entertainment, culture. Cinema 40 F; discotheque 80–100 F (drink sometimes included); Jurques Zoo 40 F, children (3–12 years) 25 F Bayeux Tapestry 28 F, under-16s 13 F, children under 10 free.

Hairdressers. *Man's* haircut 50–80 F, cut/wash/style 70–100 F *Woman's* wash/blow dry 80 F, cut/colour 150–200 F.

Hotels (double room). **** 800–1200 F, *** 300–700 F, ** 250–400 F * 150–250 F.

Meals and drinks. Breakfast (croissants/bread, butter, coffee) from 30 F; lunch or dinner (fixed four- or five-course menu) 90–100 F and up; crêpes (various fillings) 15 F and up. Cider (small bottle) 15 F. Wine (¼ litre *pichet*) 15 F, bottle (¾ l.) 50–500 F and up; coffee (black) 7 F (with milk) 10 F.

Riding. 80–100 F an hour, 2–3 hours' riding, overnight accommodation 300 F.

Taxes. TVA (value-added tax) 18.6% on all, 33% on luxury goods.

Taxis. Generally 11 F to start 2.79 F per km. (double if taxi return empty).

Youth hostels. 55 F a night, breakfast included.

An A–Z Summary of Practical Information and Facts

> Listed after some entries is the appropriate French translation, usually in the singular, plus a number of phrases that should help you when seeking assistance.

ACCOMMODATION (see also CAMPING). There are more than 800 classified hotels, over a third of them two-star rated and generally comfortable and clean. The Calvados Coast boasts the most superior accommodation, with four-stars-luxury hotels—the highest rating in France—at Cabourg, Deauville and tucked a little way inland at Tourgeville. Other four-star establishments can be found at Audrieu, Caen, Honfleur, Campigny and Rouen, and there's also one in southern Normandy at Condeau.

Finding a Hotel

Hotels in Normandy are as pleasantly varied as the landscape, often appearing in delightful surroundings. Arriving after a day's driving or travelling by rail can be bliss—but it can also be a disaster in the tourist season for anyone who hasn't booked in advance. If this is the case, start looking for a hotel before the end of the afternoon—it will be safer. The *Accueil de France* desk in Tourist Offices specializes in finding hotel rooms and will help with reservations. Outside the high season, many smaller hotels close from Sunday lunchtime till Monday morning—another reason to book in advance.

If there is a restaurant attached to your hotel, it is customary to have dinner there the first night. Some hotels offer a discount for this.

Note: Throughout the region, the same names crop up—Hôtel de Normandie, Hôtel de France, Hôtel de la Gare. Even more towns will have an *Hôtel de Ville,* but don't go looking there for accommodation—it's the French name for town hall. Recommended even less are the *Hôtel de Police* and *Hôtel des Impôts* (taxes)!

Classification

Hotels are classed by the Direction du Tourisme from one-star to four-star-luxury grades. Hotels marked NN *(Nouvelles Normes)* correspond to more recently established standards of comfort. Prices, fixed according to star rating, amenities and size, should be clearly indicated at the hotel entrance or reception desk, as well as in each room on the back of the door. *Pension* (full board—all meals) can usually be

A obtained for any stay of three or more days. *Demi-pension* (half board—breakfast and evening meal) terms are usually available outside the peak holiday period.

Relais et Châteaux. These hotels, covering the whole of France, offer several tempting possibilities in the *départements* of Eure, Calvados and Manche. All are four-star establishments.

Relais du Silence. A chain of two- to four-star hotels in tranquil settings. Some are genuine, old-time stagecoach inns. Establishments are listed in a free booklet published annually, available from the tourist office.

Logis de France, Auberges de France. Small or quiet hotels, often outside or on the outskirts of towns. *Logis de France* are in the one- and two-star bracket; *Auberges de France* are typical inn-type establishments in the country. A *Guide des Logis de France* is produced annually and given out free at national tourist offices abroad.

Gîtes de France, Gîtes ruraux. Furnished holiday accommodation, with standards and prices officially controlled. Your *gîte* could be a delightful surprise: a small cottage, a village house, a flat in the owner's house or part of a farm. Weekly rental costs are inclusive of all charges. You can also stay in one of the *chambres d'hôte*—a furnished room, often on a farm, with breakfast included in the price.

And there are **Villages de Vacances** (Holiday Villages)—flats grouped together with sporting and leisure activities—as well as **Stations Vertes de Vacances** ("Green" Holiday Centres), in relaxed settings throughout Seine-Maritime.

Auberges de Jeunesse (youth hostels). Normandy has 16 hostels—more than half fully equipped, the others smaller or offering fewer facilities. Food often isn't available, although at Caen and Rouen—two of the biggest youth hostels, with 100 or more beds, open all the year round—you can get all meals. If you plan to stop at one of the smaller hostels such as Bayeux or Yvetot, it's best to ring and check whether there's still room. You can obtain further information from the Fédération Unie des Auberges de Jeunesse, 9bis, rue Brantôme, 75003 Paris, tel. 16 ~ (1) 48.04.70.40.

Do you have a single/double room for tonight?	**Avez-vous une chambre pour une/deux personnes pour cette nuit?**
with bath/shower/toilet	**avec bains/douche/toilettes**
What's the rate per night?	**Quel est le prix pour une nuit?**

BABY-SITTERS (see also CHILDREN). Hotels can often arrange for a baby-sitter, especially at resorts where beach clubs *(Clubs de plage/ loisirs)* specialize in activities for young children during the day. Otherwise, baby-sitters sometimes advertise in the local papers, under *Garderie d'enfants, Crèche* or *Halte-garderie*. The term *garde d'enfants* often applies to professional child-minders who look after children full time while their mothers are at work. You can also ask for the name of a baby-sitter at the grocer's, baker's, supermarket—or tourist office. Use the word "baby-sitter" first when inquiring—it's well understood throughout Normandy. The local tourist office can usually help if necessary.

Can you get me a baby-sitter for tonight?	**Pouvez-vous me trouver une baby-sitter pour ce soir?**

BEACHES. Summer-season swimming in Normandy is a delight. The beaches along the Côte de Nacre and Côte Fleurie, either side of Caen, are long, wide and flat. West coast sands are largely sheltered, and parts of the Cotentin peninsula are often uncrowded, even in summer. Where there is likely to be a problem with tide, currents or rocks, the beaches are patrolled—particularly at the resorts *(stations balnéaires/ estivales)*. Watch out for any red flag, which signifies danger, or a warning notice: *Baignade interdite* (swimming forbidden). A green flag flies when it's safe. If you find a smaller beach, or cove, and aren't sure of the conditions, it's best to ask someone—and not risk swimming alone.

Can we swim here?	**Peut-on se baigner ici?**

BOAT TRIPS. Summer boat trips on the Seine as it winds its way through eastern Normandy are a relaxing way of enjoying the surrounding greenery. There are day cruises from Le Havre as far as Rouen, and shorter trips, with food on board.

Further upriver, full-day and half-day excursions are organized at certain times between Amfreville-sous-les-Monts, les Andelys and Vernon.

Harbour boat trips are another possibility, particularly a tour of the forts around Cherbourg's massive port basin. From Granville, down on Normandy's west coast, you can get a boat out to the granite Chausey Islands, said to have once been part of the Scissy Forest before the sea took over. Alternatively, there are day trips to the Channel Islands (known as *les îles Anglo-Normandes*) from Granville, Carteret, Cherbourg and Goury.

C **CAMPING.** Whether on the dramatic cliffs of the Côte d'Albâtre, th shady banks of the Seine or in the gentle landscape of the *bocage* there are more than 350 camping and/or caravan sites to choose from in Normandy—all classified from one- to four-star. Most have som sporting facility on site or close by, many also hire out bicycles, and more than a third offer instant access to the Normandy coast.

You aren't allowed to camp on public land outside official sites— what's known as *"camping sauvage"*—although you may put up a tent on private property if you have the owner's permission. Look ou for two signs: *Camping à la ferme*, which means you can camp on th farmer's land, and *Camping interdit*—no camping allowed.

Have you room for a tent/a caravan?	**Avez-vous de la place pour une tente/une caravane?**
May we camp on your land, please?	**Pouvons-nous camper sur votre terrain, s'il vous plaît?**

CAR HIRE *(location de voitures).* Car-hire firms throughout Nor mandy handle French and foreign makes. Local firms sometimes offe lower prices than the international companies.

To hire a car you must show your driving licence (held for at leas one year) and passport. The minimum age for hiring cars is from 20 to 23—even 25 or 30 if a particularly expensive car is involved. A sub stantial deposit (refundable) is usually required unless you hold a credit card recognized by the car-hire company.

I'd like to hire a car now/ tomorrow.	**Je voudrais louer une voiture tout de suite/demain.**
for one day/a week	**pour une journée/une semaine**

CHILDREN. From start to finish, youngsters are on to a winner Apart from their own tailor-made entertainment, many of the adul attractions will fascinate them too. The Mont-Saint-Michel, fo example, is as impressive a castle in the sand as any child could wish for. The eerie shapes of the chalk cliffs at Etretat or the lighthouse of Gatteville (Val de Saire) and Goury (Hague), are also interesting to children. Then there are the war museums at Avranches, Cherbourg Sainte-Mère-Eglise, Sainte-Marie-du-Mont, Arromanches, Bayeux

Ouistreham-Riva-Bella, Bénouville and Caen (Mémorial de la Paix)

Once this list is exhausted—and the children aren't—you can send them down a coal mine (le Molay-Littry), hoist them into an air balloon (Château de Balleroy) or pack them on a steam train (Thévray). More conventional, but just as inviting, are the aquarium at Trouville, the Museum of the Sea at Courseulles-sur-Mer and a perennial attraction, the zoo, at Jurques, Champrepus or Clères. Other animals can be seen roaming in parks at Champeaux and St-Symphorien-des-Monts.

During the summer, there are sound and light *(son et lumière)* presentations at Gavray and Saint-Laurent-de-Terregatte. In good weather, parks and playgrounds are plentiful—Rouen's Botanical Garden is a riot of colour, and both Longny and Vimoutiers have play areas with swimming pools and other activities. Not to mention the wide selection of beach clubs, where entertainment in all weather for children of all ages is a priority.

CLOTHING. The ideal outfit: cautious summer wear with thick jumper and anorak to back it up. All-purpose shoes are a must, suntan cream will help soothe any stinging from the wind, and don't forget to take an umbrella.

The weather can change, but in any case the fascination of Normandy far outweighs any temporary aberration of climate. If you get caught in the rain, bear it stoically and remember the optimism of this French proverb: *La pluie du matin n'arrête pas le pèlerin;* which, loosely translated, means: It can only get better.

COMMUNICATIONS

Post office. French post offices display a sign with a stylized blue bird and/or the words *Postes et Télécommunications, P&T* or *la Poste*.

In addition to normal mail service, you can make local or long-distance telephone calls, send telegrams and receive or send money at any post office.

Note: You can also buy stamps *(timbres)* at a tobacconists and, occasionally, at hotels and from postcard or souvenir vendors.

Poste restante (general delivery). If you don't know ahead of time where you'll be staying, you can have your mail addressed to you in any town c/o *Poste restante, Poste centrale.* You can collect it only on presentation of your passport. A small fee is charged. If you're British, are expecting a business letter and find none, try asking the counter clerk to look under E for "Esquire"... Yes, it does happen.

Telegrams. All local post offices accept inland and overseas telegrams. You may also dictate a telegram over the phone (dial 14), and as one **109**

C of the French Post Office's special services, a telegram can be handed in up to ten days before you want it sent. Reply-paid telegrams *(réponse payée)* are accepted by post offices and, if you require, you can be notified of the time of arrival when sending a telegram.

Telephone *(téléphone)*. Long-distance and international calls can be made from any phone box, but if you need assistance in placing the call, go to the post office or get your hotel to do it. If you want to make a reverse-charge (collect) call, ask for *un appel en PCV* (pronounced: pay-say-vay). For a personal (person-to-person) call, specify *un appel avec préavis pour…*

Taxiphone isn't for taxis—it's a normal telephone, just like any phone box *(cabine téléphonique)* you'll find in Normandy.

Coin-operated phones no longer take 20-centime coins; you can use ½-franc, 1-franc, 5-franc and sometimes 2-franc coins. Some phone boxes take a *télécarte,* a form of credit card available from post offices, railway ticket counters and shops recognized by a "Télécarte" sign, and are valid for 40 or 120 charge units. If you telephone from your hotel, you are likely to be charged a little extra.

To make an international call, dial 19 and wait for a continuous burring tone before dialling the rest of the number. Here are the full codes for the main English-speaking countries:

Australia	19…61	South Africa	19…27
Canada	19…1	United Kingdom	19…44
Irish Republic	19…35	United States	19…1
New Zealand	19…64		

If you want international inquiries, put 33 between the 19 and the code of the country for which you need to know the number, e.g. 19–33 44 (inquiries for the U.K.). For inquiries concerning the U.S. or Canada, dial 11 instead of 1 (19–33 11).

For long-distance calls within France, there are no area codes (just dial the 8-digit number of the person you want to call), *except* when telephoning from Paris or the Paris region (Ile-de-France) to the provinces (dial 16 and wait for the dialling tone, then dial the 8-digit number of the subscriber) and from the provinces to Paris or the Ile-de-France (dial 16, wait for the dialling tone, then dial 1 followed by the 8-digit number). If all else fails, call the operator for help (12).

express (special delivery)	**par exprès**
airmail	**par avion**
registered	**en recommandé**

110 Have you any mail for …? **Avez-vous du courrier pour …?**

COMPLAINTS. In general, try not to complain about minor things—it will do more harm than good, particularly if your French isn't fluent enough and your self-confidence steady enough. Take inadequacies with tolerance, tact and the realization that nobody's perfect, even the French. But if something goes seriously wrong, don't hesitate to complain, at the same time observing three golden rules: do it on the spot, calmly, and to the correct person. At a hotel or restaurant this will be the manager *(maître d'hôtel* or *directeur).* In extreme cases, a police station *(Commissariat de Police)* may help or, failing that, the regional administration offices *(Préfecture* ou *Sous-Préfecture).* Ask for the *Service du Tourisme.* If you should have reason to complain, firmness, a sense of humour and a little French are your most useful assets.

I'd like to make a complaint.   **J'ai une réclamation à faire.**

CONSULATES and EMBASSIES. Contact your consulate or embassy when in trouble (loss of passport, theft or loss of all your money, problems with the police, serious accident). The nearest British consulate is at Dinard, in neighbouring Brittany. Citizens of other English-speaking countries should get in touch with their representatives in Paris.

Australia (embassy and consulate): 4, rue Jean-Rey, 75015 Paris; tel. 16~ (1) 40.59.33.00.

Canada (embassy): 35, avenue Montaigne, 75008 Paris; tel. 16~ (1) 47.23.01.01.

Irish Republic (embassy): 12, avenue Foch (enter from 4, rue Rude), 75016 Paris; tel. 16~ (1) 45.00.20.87.

New Zealand (embassy-chancellery): 7ter, rue Léonard-de-Vinci, 75116 Paris; tel. 16~ (1) 45.00.24.11.

South Africa (chancellery-consulate): 59, quai d'Orsay, 75007 Paris; tel. 16~ (1) 45.55.92.37.

United Kingdom (consulate): 8, avenue de la Libération, 35800 Dinard; tel. 99.46.26.64; (embassy): 35, Faubourg-Saint-Honoré, 75008 Paris; tel. 16~ (1) 42.66.91.42.

U.S. (embassy): 2, rue Saint-Florentin, 75001 Paris; tel. 16~ (1) 42.96.14.88.

CONVERSION CHARTS. For distance and fluid measures, se p. 115. France uses the metric system.

Length

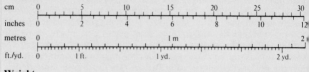

Weight

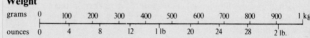

CRIME and THEFT. Watch your wallet and handbag, especially i crowds. Keep items of value in your hotel safe and obtain a receipt fc them. It's a good idea to leave any large amounts of money there a well.

Lock your car at all times and leave nothing valuable inside. The ca parks at seaside lookout points are classic targets for thieves. Any los or theft should be reported at once to the nearest *Commissariat a Police.*

I want to report a theft.	**Je voudrais signaler un vol.**
My ticket/wallet/passport/ handbag/credit card has been stolen.	**On m'a volé mon billet/porte- feuille/passeport/sac à main/ (ma) carte de crédit.**

CYCLING. The charm of Normandy's ever-changing countryside ca be enjoyed to the full on two wheels. Cycles can be hired at railwa stations, tourist offices, camp sites or bicycle shops in well over 5 towns and villages. One advantage of hiring a bike from the Frenc Railways (SNCF) is that you can leave it at another station—useful i you're in a hilly area, or want to cycle as far as possible without goin back on yourself. But this isn't a problem if you're in a flat region lik Seine-Maritime, where you can also arrange a "package" that cover both the hire of the bike and overnight accommodation along a spe cially designated route.

Several towns also have **mopeds** *(vélomoteurs)* for hire, and it's possible to hire scooters (same word in French) in Rouen.

All moped and motorcycle riders and passengers must wear crash helmets. Use of dipped headlights is obligatory at all times of day. Mopeds are not allowed on motorways.

I'd like to hire a bicycle/ moped/scooter.	**Je voudrais louer une bicyclette/ un vélomoteur/scooter.**
for one day/a week	**pour une journée/une semaine**

DRIVING IN FRANCE. To take a car into France, you will need:

   A valid driving licence
 ● Car registration papers
   Insurance coverage (the green card is no longer obligatory but comprehensive coverage is advisable)
   A red warning triangle and a set of spare bulbs

Drivers and front-seat passengers are required by law to wear seat belts. Children under 10 may not travel in the front (unless the car has no back seat). Driving on a foreign provisional licence is not permitted in France. Minimum age is 18.

Driving regulations: Drive on the right, overtake on the left. (*Serrez à droite* means "keep to the right".) British drivers should be careful not to forget momentarily that they should be driving on the right, such as when they emerge from a one-way street, a refuelling stop, at a T-junction or when turning left at traffic lights. In built-up areas, give automatic priority to vehicles coming from the right. The priority will be taken in any case so it's only wise to "offer" it first. But the *priorité* rule does not apply at roundabouts (traffic circles). Outside built-up areas—at junctions marked by signs with a cross or a yellow square on a white background—the more important of two roads has right of way. The use of car horns in built-up areas is allowed only as a warning. At night, lights should be used for this purpose.

Speed limits: On dry roads, 130 kph (around 80 mph) on toll motorways (expressways), 110 kph (68 mph) on dual carriageways (divided highways), 90 kph (56 mph) on other country roads, and 45 or 50 kph (28 or 37 mph) in built-up areas. *Note:* when roads are wet, all limits are reduced by 10 kph (6 mph), except for motorways—where maximum speed in fog, rain or snow is reduced by 20 kph (12 mph). The word *rappel* in towns and villages reminds you that a speed limit is in force.

D **Signposting** is much better than it used to be—particularly in an around towns—but in country areas you'll more often than not have to rely on a good map or the locals.

A blue road sign directs you to an *autoroute* (motorway), a green one to a *route nationale* (*RN*—main road) and white to secondary roads (those maintained by the *département* concerned).

Road conditions. The more voluble Norman will cheerfully deride the state of the roads in his region, insisting that they are even worse than the government of the day. To be fair, neither is all that bad. The A1 motorway sweeps through the heart of Normandy from Paris, taking you effortlessly to Caen, and there are many other good stretches of road between towns. But don't expect this wherever you go—in the countryside it can be very different. The winding roads of the Suisse Normande around Thury-Harcourt, Clécy and Pont-d'Ouilly are justifiably known as *routes accidentées*—high-risk roads with tricky bends and sudden dips that can take you by surprise. Here, as in many other places, conditions are not suitable for speed. But then Normandy isn't a region to hurry through.

You can get the latest information on road conditions in Seine-Maritime and Eure by ringing 20.47.33.33 (Lille). For information on roads in Calvados, Manche and Orne ring 99.32.33.33 (Rennes). France-Inter's *Inter-Route* service—which operates 24 hours a day from Paris—can also help. Most of the time, there is someone who speaks English. Phone (1) 48.58.33.33. Then there's the Centre d'Information Autoroutes, 7 bis, rue du Pont des Loges, 55007 Paris, tel. 16 ~ (1) 47.05.90.01.

Parking *(stationnement).* You'll encounter two systems of parking—*zone bleue* (blue zone) and meters. If you want to leave your car in *zone bleue* you will need a *disque de stationnement,* a parking disc in the form of a cardboard clock which you can get from a petrol station newsagent or stationer. Set it to show the time you arrived and it will indicate when you have to leave. Then display it in the car, visible through the windscreen. *Disque obligatoire* means "Disc obligatory".

Stationnement interdit means "No parking". Above all, don't leave your car in a *Zone piétonne* (Pedestrian precinct), even less if the sign says *Stationnement gênant* (Parking obstructive). Here, translation is superfluous and language neither a barrier nor excuse—an accompanying pictograph shows your car's fate: being towed away.

Breakdowns. One piece of advice you may get in Normandy about breaking down is: don't do it on a Sunday. But despite the gloom mplication, all is not lost for those who do. Dial 17, wherever you are, and the police can put you in touch with a garage that will come to your rescue. At a price, of course—so it's wise to take out an international breakdown insurance before leaving home. Local garages usually provide towing facilities and spare parts for European cars. Always ask for an estimate before authorizing repairs, and expect to pay TVA (value-added tax) on top of the cost.

Fuel and oil *(essence; huile)*: Fuel is available in super (98 octane), normal (90 octane), lead-free (95 octane) and diesel *(gas-oil)*. It's customary to give a tip if someone checks your tyre pressures.

Fluid measures

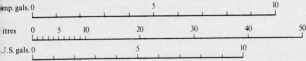

Distance

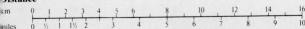

Road signs: Most road signs are the standard international pictographs, but you may encounter these written signs as well:

Accotements non stabilisés	Soft shoulders
Chaussée déformée	Uneven road surface
Déviation	Diversion (detour)
Gravillons	Loose gravel
Péage	Toll
Priorité à droite	Yield to traffic from right
Ralentir	Slow down
Serrez à droite/à gauche	Keep right/left
driving licence	**permis de conduire**
car registration papers	**carte grise**
Are we on the right road for ...?	**Sommes-nous sur la route de ...?**
Fill the tank, please.	**Le plein, s'il vous plaît.**
lead-free/normal/super	**sans plomb/normale/super**
I've had a breakdown.	**Ma voiture est en panne.**
There's been an accident.	**Il y a eu un accident.**

115

E   **EMERGENCIES** *(urgence)*. You can get assistance anywhere in France by dialling 17 for the police *(police secours)*; 18 for the fire brigade *(pompiers)*, who also turn out for medical emergencies.

Careful!	**Attention!**	Police!	**Police!**
Fire!	**Au feu!**	Stop, thief!	**Au voleur!**
Help!	**Au secours!**		

Can you help me?   **Pouvez-vous m'aider?**

ENTRY FORMALITIES and CUSTOMS *(douane)*. British visitors need only a passport to enter France, as do nationals of other EC countries and Switzerland. Anyone else should contact the French embassy in his or her country for the latest information on entry requirements.

The following chart shows some main items you may take into France and, when returning home, into your own country:

Into:	Cigarettes		Cigars		Tobacco	Liquor		Wine
France 1)	200	or	50	or	250 g.	1 l.	and	2 l.
2)	800	and	200	and	1 kg.	10 l.	and	90 l.
3)	400	or	100	or	500 g.	1 l.	and	2 l.
Canada	200	and	50	and	900 g.	1.1 l.	or	1 l.
Eire 1)	200	or	50	or	250 g.	1 l.	and	2 l.
2)	800	and	200	and	1 kg.	10 l.	and	90 l.
U.K. 1)	200	or	50	or	250 g.	1 l.	and	2 l.
2)	800	and	200	and	1 kg.	10 l.	and	90 l.
U.S.A.	200	and	100	and	4)	1 l.	or	1 l.

1) Arriving from EC countries (and items have been purchased duty free) or from other European countries.
2) Arriving from EC countries (and duty has been paid on items).
3) Residents outside Europe.
4) A reasonable quantity.

British visitors may also bring back from France £120 worth of goods duty free.

Currency restrictions: There's no limit on the importation or exportation of local or foreign currencies or traveller's cheques, but amounts exceeding 50,000 French francs or equivalent must be declared on arrival.

I've nothing to declare.	**Je n'ai rien à déclarer.**
It's for my own use.	**C'est pour mon usage personnel.**

GETTING AROUND

Train. With the right planning, this can be quite an effective and relaxing means of covering Normandy. You can reach Pontorson (for the Mont-Saint-Michel) and Granville direct from Paris's Montparnasse station, cutting across the southern part of the region. Alternatively, you can get down there from Cherbourg, via Lison—although the journey is rather complicated. Rail connections to Caen, for the D-Day beaches and Bayeux, are good from most parts of the region as well as from Paris (St-Lazare station).

Bus. City buses *(service urbain)* and linking services *(service interurbain)* are an efficient form of transport for sightseeing. The *bus verts* (green buses) of Caen are particularly useful, ferrying passengers to all parts of the Calvados Coast and the D-Day beaches. Certain tickets are obtainable at reduced rates. Details are available from the bus station *(gare routière)*, near Caen railway station. You can also ring this number for information (they speak English): 31.44.77.44. SNCF bus excursions are organized from Cherbourg to Bayeux, the D-Day beaches and the Mont-Saint-Michel.

Car (see also DRIVING). Thanks to the A13 motorway, much of Normandy is readily accessible by road. From the end of the A13, if you're driving up the Cotentin peninsula, the RN13 can become a bit of a headache because of all the lorries and caravans heading for the Cherbourg ferries. But after Montebourg, the four-lane road makes passing easier. A picturesque—and good—route down from Les Pieux, in the north-west, will take you to Granville in an hour and a half, well within reach of the Mont-Saint-Michel.

To give you more idea of the ground you can cover, here are a few approximate distances in kilometres (miles in brackets) from Caen to other major towns, ports or points of interest: Alençon 101 (63), Bayeux 27 (17), Cherbourg 119 (74), Dieppe 182 (113), Evreux 121 (75), Le Havre 109 (68), the Mont-Saint-Michel 130 (81), Rouen 124 (77).

G **Plane.** Regular flights connect Caen and Le Havre throughout th year and you can also fly from Rouen to Lisieux, via Nantes. Ai taxi services operate from five airports—Caen, Deauville, Granville Le Havre and Rouen.

Taxi. You'll find metered taxis in all Normandy towns. They are liste under "Taxis" in the local telephone directory. If your ride takes yo out of town, you usually have to pay for the return journey even if yo aren't coming back in the taxi. There is an extra charge for baggag Some taxis are not insured to take more than three passengers.

H **HOURS OF OPENING** (heures d'ouverture)

Banks tend to open from 9 a.m. to 5 p.m. on weekdays (many closin for lunch from 12 till 2) and close either on Saturdays (main towns) o Mondays. All banks close on major national or regional holidays an most close early on the day preceding a public holiday.

Main post offices: 8 a.m.–7 p.m. weekdays, 8 a.m.–noon Saturday Post offices in smaller towns usually close for lunch from 12 till 2 2.30 p.m., as well as shutting for the day at 5 or 6 p.m.

Groceries, bakeries, food shops: 7 a.m.–7 p.m. Monday–Saturday Food shops are often open on Sunday mornings—bakeries, butchers charcuteries, in particular, but also some supermarkets. Lunchtim closing, from 12.30 to 2, 2.30 or even 3 p.m., is the norm for sma shops.

Other shops: Generally 9 or 9.30 a.m.–6.30 or 7 p.m. Tuesday t Saturday, closing Monday morning or all day.

Museums, châteaux, monuments: 10 a.m. (variable)–5.30 p.m. (vari able). Closing day is usually Tuesday, but not always. It's best to chec before going. During low season, many close or have reduced hours

L **LANGUAGE.** Most older people you meet will consider themselve 1) Norman and 2) French, in that order. The distinction is impor tant—although there is no Norman language as such, words lik "patois" and "dialect" don't go down too well. The "local languages (parlers locaux) as they're known, are spoken in no fewer than six di ferent forms throughout Normandy. Each area guards its own expres sions and individual pronunciation of standard French words.

There are some quaint departures from modern-day French which rather than being distortions, stay closer to the original Latin or Ge man sounds. The aspirate H is often pronounced in Normandy, like *hamé* instead of h*ameau* (hamlet). The *sh* sound of the French ch can become *tch*, as in tchu nous—chez nous (at our place).

If you see a *larderie*, it's another way of saying *charcuterie* (pork butcher) in the Cherbourg area. A *moque* is a Norman word for a cider mug, and a *bon bère* is a good cider.

Here are a few regional peculiarities (standard French equivalents in brackets) that still come up in conversations among fishermen and farmers:

bère (boire)	to drink	**pon** (poire)	pear
bouès (bois)	wood	**péyi** (pain)	bread
boutèle (bouteille)	bottle	**pouès** (pays)	country
		viage (voyage)	journey
byin (bien)	well		
cat (chat)	cat	**cnâle** (enfant)	child
canchon (chanson)	song	**horzin** (étranger)	stranger/ foreigner
chent (cent)	hundred	**pièce** (rien)	nothing
jonne (jeune)	young	**tchique** (quelque)	some
mâquer/mangi (manger)	to eat	**û miot** (un peu)	a little
mé (mer, moi)	sea, me	**vêtu** (porc)	pig

The Berlitz phrase book FRENCH FOR TRAVELLERS covers almost all situations you're likely to encounter on your travels in France. If further help is required, the Berlitz French-English/English-French pocket dictionary contains the basic vocabulary a tourist will need, plus a menu-reader supplement.

Goodbye.	**Au revoir.**
You're welcome.	**Je vous en prie.**
Speak slowly, please.	**Parlez lentement, s'il vous plaît.**
I didn't understand.	**Je n'ai pas compris.**

MEDICAL CARE. (See also EMERGENCIES.) Make sure your health insurance policy covers illness or accident while on holiday. If not, ask your insurance representative, motoring association or travel agent about special holiday insurance plans.

Visitors from EEC countries with corresponding health insurance facilities are entitled to medical and hospital treatment under the French social security system. Before leaving home, ensure that you are eligible and have the appropriate forms required to obtain this **119**

M benefit in case of need. Doctors who belong to the French social security system *(médecins conventionnés)* charge the minimum.

If you're taken ill or have a toothache, your hotel receptionist can probably recommend an English-speaking doctor or dentist; otherwise ask at the *Syndicat d'Initiative,* or in an emergency the *gendarmerie.*

Chemists *(pharmacies)* display green crosses. Staff are helpful in dealing with minor ailments and can recommend a nurse *(infirmière)* if you need injections or other special care. In towns throughout Normandy, there'll be a chemist on duty at night on a rota system *(service de garde)*. The name and address of the duty chemist is displayed in the window of other pharmacies. Otherwise, you can get it from the *gendarmerie* or the local papers. *Ouest-France* lists chemists and doctors on call *(pharmaciens/médecins de garde)* in regional editions (Manche, Orne and Calvados departments) under its "Le week-end" or "Aujourd'hui" column. *Paris-Normandie* (Eure and Seine-Maritime) does the same under "A Votre Service".

MEETING PEOPLE. The taciturn Normans may be in two minds about living in "la dernière solitude de France"—so near to Paris yet so far. That's how they see their region, finding little in common with the many Parisians who pass through on their way to the resorts and their weekend cottages. But then, it works both ways: Normans may feel overlooked, but they take a quiet satisfaction in retaining their privacy and traditions. They are proud and rather shy, on their guard against the unknown, yet happy to open up this oyster-like exterior in the face of courtesy, genuine interest and an attempt to speak their language. But if they are less spontaneous than their counterparts in the South of France, they do at least make the effort to speak English—a gesture that in a Frenchman is some concession indeed. Two subjects are calculated to draw out the Normans—politics and the English.

Their sense of isolation is as much a product of environment as culture. Even at the height of summer, as thousands of holiday-makers are indulging themselves in Normandy's international-style hotels, spas and fashionable resorts, you can still find yourself alone on a 10-kilometre stretch of sand at Calvaire des Dunes on the western Manche. Many Normans would like to keep it that way.

French people shake hands when greeting each other or saying goodbye, a formality repeated on each subsequent occasion. When you're introduced to someone or meeting an acquaintance, do the same. Friends kiss on the cheeks once, twice, three times or—if they are young—as many as four times.

MONEY MATTERS

Currency. The French *franc* (abbreviated F or FF) is divided into 100 *centimes* (ct.).

Coins: 5, 10, 20, 50 ct.; 1, 2, 5, 10 F.
Banknotes: 20, 50, 100, 200, 500 F.

For currency restrictions, see ENTRY FORMALITIES AND CUSTOMS.

Banks and currency exchange. (See also HOURS.) Local tourist offices *may* change money outside banking hours at the official bank rate. Take your passport when you go to change money or traveller's cheques. Your hotel may also come to the rescue, though you'll get a less favourable rate of exchange. The same applies to foreign currency or traveller's cheques changed in stores, boutiques or restaurants.

Credit cards are being used in an increasing number of hotels, restaurants, shops and service stations, as well as for obtaining money from cash dispensers *(distributeurs automatiques)*.

Traveller's cheques and Eurocheques are widely accepted throughout France. Outside the towns, it's preferable to have some ready cash with you.

Sales tax. A value-added tax called TVA is imposed on almost all goods and services. In hotels and restaurants, this is accompanied by a service charge.

Visitors from non-EEC countries will be refunded the TVA on larger purchases. Ask the sales assistant for the requisite form, to be filled out and handed to French customs on departure.

Where's the nearest bank/currency exchange office?	**Où se trouve la banque/le bureau de change la/le plus proche?**
I want to change some pounds/dollars.	**Je voudrais changer des livres sterling/des dollars.**
Do you accept traveller's cheques/this credit card?	**Acceptez-vous les chèques de voyage/cette carte de crédit?**

NEWSPAPERS and MAGAZINES *(journaux; magazines).* During the tourist season, you can be pretty certain—barring a strike at one end or the other—of getting major British and other European newspapers and news magazines on publication day or the following morning. The Paris edition of the *International Herald Tribune* is available at main newsagents in resorts and larger towns. Local editions of one or other of the two regional daily newspapers, *Ouest-*

N *France* and *Paris-Normandie,* are on sale in all main towns. These as well as the local papers, contain up-to-date information on events entertainment and sporting activities.

P **POLICE.** In cities and larger towns, you'll see the blue-uniforme *police municipale;* they are the local police force who direct traffic keep order and investigate crime.

Outside the main towns are the *gendarmes;* they wear blue trouser and black jackets with white belts and are responsible for traffic an crime investigation. They are usually pleasant, helpful and efficien but not many speak English.

PUBLIC HOLIDAYS *(jours fériés).* These are France's national holi days. If one of them falls on a Tuesday or Thursday, many Frenc people take the Monday or Friday off as well to make a long weeken (but this doesn't usually affect shops or businesses).

January 1	*Jour de l'An*	New Year's Day
May 1	*Fête du Travail*	Labour Day
May 8	*Fête de la Victoire 1945*	Victory Day
July 14	*Fête nationale*	Bastille Day
August 15	*Assomption*	Assumption
November 1	*Toussaint*	All Saints' Day
November 11	*Armistice*	Armistice Day (1918)
December 25	*Noël*	Christmas Day
Movable dates:	*Lundi de Pâques*	Easter Monday
	Ascension	Ascension
	Lundi de Pentecôte	Whit Monday

In France, school holidays vary from region to region but, as else where, resorts tend to fill up in the summer. In general, children' summer holidays begin in late June and go on to early September August can be appallingly crowded in big centres and on the mor popular beaches.

Are you open tomorrow? **Est-ce que vous ouvrez demain?**

R **RIDING.** The Norman passion for horse-riding—together with th region's fame in horse-breeding—is a throwback to the days of th Vikings, who practically revered the animal. Riding centres hav

now mushroomed to more than 80, and you can arrange holidays an weekends on horseback as well as hiring horses and ponies by the day or half-day. One related form of transport gaining popularity, if not speed, is the horse-drawn gypsy caravan *(roulotte)*. In Calvados, a group of some 30 hoteliers offer special terms and provide facilities geared to horse-riding, cycling and walking weekends.

For details about the riding centres *(centres équestres)*, contact the Fédération Equestre Française (FEF), Ligue de Normandie: 235, rue Caponière, BP 6092, 14063 Caen Cedex; tel. 31.73.31.35.

THALASSOTHERAPY. The treatment of various ailments using processes involving sea water, sea mud and other elements is available at thalassotherapy centres *(stations thalassothérapie)* along the Normandy coast. The centres—such as those at Ouistreham, Dieppe, Trouville, Deauville, Luc-sur-Mer, Siouville-Hague and Granville—specialize in a number of problem areas including anaemia, cellulitis, poor circulation, obesity, rheumatism and therapy/convalescence following accidents or surgery.

In addition, there are standard thermal spas *(stations thermales)* which use river waters, inland at Forges-les-Eaux and Bagnoles-de-l'Orne/Tessé-la-Madeleine for blood circulation.

You can get details from the Comité Régional du Tourisme de Normandie, Le Doyenné, 14, rue Charles-Corbeau, F-27000 Evreux; tel. 32.33.79.00; fax 32.31.19.04.

TIME DIFFERENCES. France keeps to Central European Time (GMT + 1). Summer time (GMT + 2) comes into force from late March to end September. The days are long at the height of summer, when it's still light at 11 p.m. The following chart gives summer time differences.

New York	London	**France**	Sydney	Auckland
6 a.m.	11 a.m.	**noon**	8 p.m.	10 p.m.

What time is it?   **Quelle heure est-il?**

TIPPING. A little tip can go a long way in Normandy, all the more so now that the practice is dying out as a result of inexorable inflation. In the main, the tip has been incorporated into restaurant prices—a canny way of looking after your conscience for you. If the prices aren't inclusive *(service non compris)*, you can add up to 10 percent to your bill:

T

Hotel porter, per bag	4–5 F
Hotel maid, per week	50–100 F
Lavatory attendant	2 F
Waiter	5–10% (optional)
Taxi driver	10–15%
Hairdresser/Barber	15% (gen. incl.)
Tour guide	10%

TOILETS. Regular visitors to France will notice that remarkable progress has been in recent years. Many toilets are now fully equipped—most with toilet seats (occasionally removable, according to the custom), toilet paper, wash basins and even soap. The range of up-to-date accoutrements can take even the most cynical by surprise. There are still, of course, hiccups in the system. At the other end of the scale the unholy "footprints" are still to be found, the door may not close (luckily, Normans show laudable aplomb), and toilet paper may be found wanting. The light probably won't work either, in which case be thankful for small mercies.

In an ideal world, *"Hommes"* or *"Messieurs"* stand for "Men" and *"Dames"* is for "Ladies", but if there's nothing to show which is which, just take pot luck. Even when the doors are marked (often with a pictograph), the distinction is not of any particular importance to the average French man or woman.

Where are the toilets, please? **Où sont les toilettes, s'il vous plaît?**

TOURIST INFORMATION OFFICES. Before going to Normandy you can get a great deal of useful information from a national tourist office abroad. Once you arrive, head for the local tourist office—the *Syndicat d'Initiative (S.I.)* or *Office de Tourisme*—usually situated close to the railway station or port. Either may be signposted by the internationally recognized form of I (Information).

Generally, the *Syndicat d'Initiative,* in smaller towns, gives information on more local places of interest, while the bigger *Office de Tourisme* will provide details on the whole region—and can book accommodation and change foreign currency. Tourist office staff usually go to great pains to help visitors with up-to-date information.

on prices, transport and other matters, as well as giving advice on what places to visit and how and when to go. They don't recommend restaurants—at least, not officially.

Hours vary, but in the summer most tourist offices open every day except Sunday from 9 or 9.30 a.m. till 12 or 1 p.m., and again from 1 or 2 p.m. till 6 or 6.30. Out of season, hours are limited and many *Syndicats d'Initiative* close.

There are French National Tourist Offices in the following English-speaking countries:

Australia	Kindersley House, 33 Bligh Street, Sydney, NSW 2000; tel. (2) 231-5244
Canada	1981 Avenue McGill College, Suite 490, Esso Tower, Montreal, Que. H3 A2 W9; tel. (514) 288-4264
	1, Dundas Street West, Suite 2405, Box 8, Toronto, Ont. M5 G1 Z3; tel. (416) 593-4717
South Africa	Carlton Centre, 10th Floor, P.O. Box 1081, Johannesburg 2000; tel. (11) 331.9252
United Kingdom	178 Piccadilly, London W1V OAL; tel. (071) 491-7622
U.S.A.	610 Fifth Avenue, New York, NY 10020; tel. (212) 757-1125
	645 North Michigan Avenue, Suite 630, Chicago, Illinois 60611; tel. (312) 337-6301
	9401 Wilshire Boulevard, Beverly Hills, California 90212; tel. (213) 272-2661
	1 Hallidie Plaza, San Francisco, California 94102; tel. (415) 986-4174
	World Trade Center, N103, 2050 Stemmons Freeway, P.O. Box 58610, Dallas, Texas 75258; tel. (214) 742-7011

WALKING. Organized weekend walks have been developed in Seine-Maritime. The routes aren't too strenuous, and a good dinner along the way helps shake off any weariness and prepare you for the next day. The walks, led by a guide, include accommodation and, usually, a visit to a place of historical or other interest.

Independent walkers are catered for by certain hotels in Calvados. Picnic baskets are prepared, and the hotels are often an enjoyable meeting-point for holiday hikers. The official "Topo" ("topographical") guides enable you to find your way around easily.

SOME USEFUL EXPRESSIONS

yes/no	oui/non
please/thank you	s'il vous plaît/merci
excuse me	excusez-moi
you're welcome	je vous en prie
where/when/how	où/quand/comment
how long/how far	combien de temps/à quelle distance
yesterday/today/tomorrow	hier/aujourd'hui/demain
day/week/month/year	jour/semaine/mois/année
left/right	gauche/droite
up/down	en haut/en bas
good/bad	bon/mauvais
big/small	grand/petit
cheap/expensive	bon marché/cher
hot/cold	chaud/froid
old/new	vieux/neuf
open/closed	ouvert/fermé
here/there	ici/là
free (vacant)/occupied	libre/occupé
early/late	tôt/tard
easy/difficult	facile/difficile

Does anyone here speak English?	Y a-t-il quelqu'un ici qui parle anglais?
What does this mean?	Que signifie ceci?
I don't understand.	Je ne comprends pas.
Please write it down.	Ecrivez-le-moi, s'il vous plaît.
Is there an admission charge?	Faut-il payer pour entrer?
Waiter/Waitress, please!	S'il vous plaît!
I'd like...	J'aimerais...
How much is that?	C'est combien?
Have you something less expensive?	Avez-vous quelque chose de moins cher?
What time is it?	Quelle heure est-il?
Help me please.	Aidez-moi, s'il vous plaît.

Index

An asterisk (*) after a page number indicates a page reference. Where there is more than one set of page references, the one in bold type refers to the main entry.